I0478662

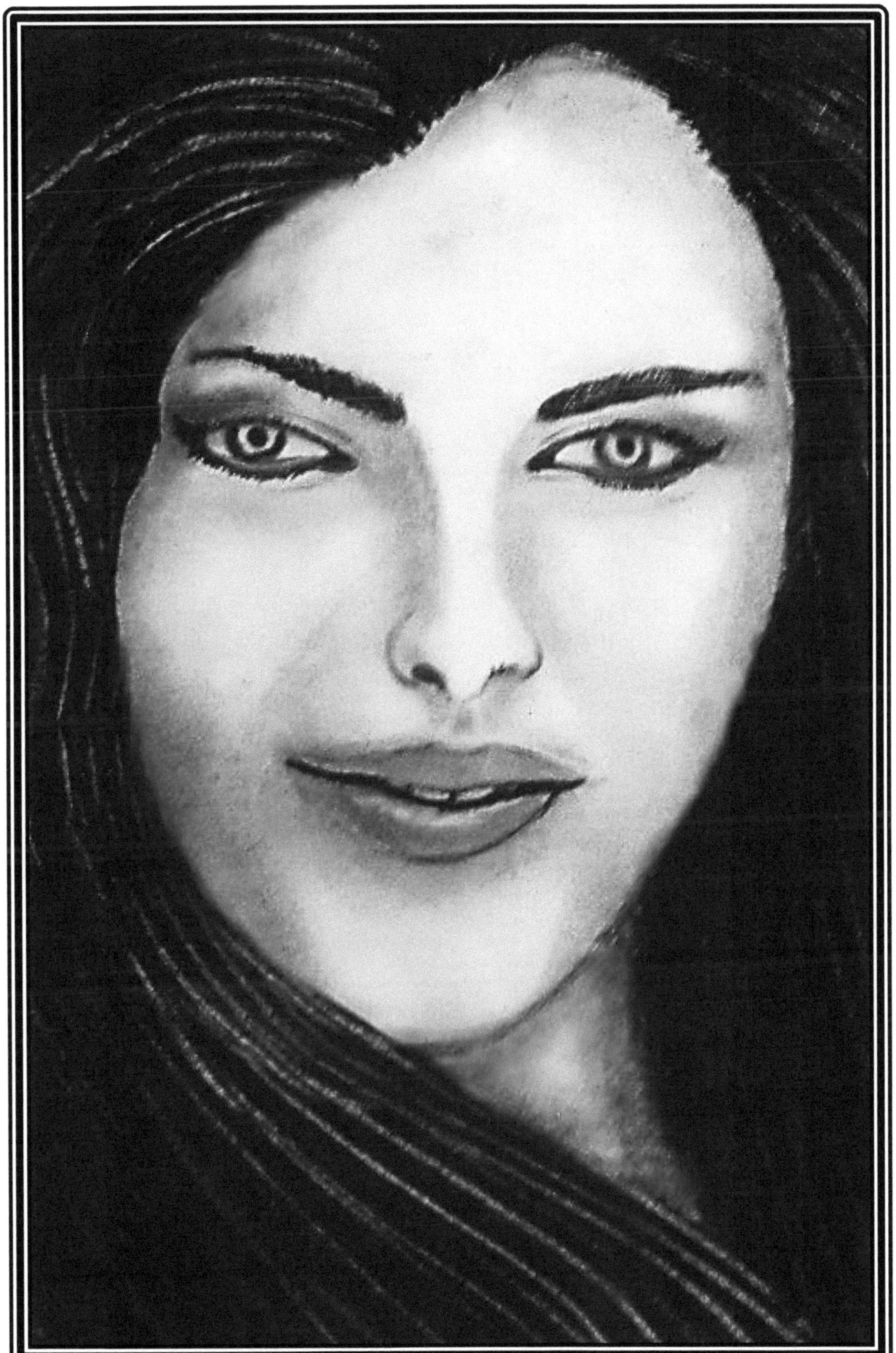

Teach Anyone

To Draw In One Hour

Forgotten

Art Technique

Book #1

Faces

Artist Jessie J. De La Portillo

Printed in the United States of America

First Printing, 2015

ISBN-13: 978-1515149781

ISBN-10:1515149781

Trilogy Light Publisher
15505 SW 138th Ave
Miami, FL 33177

Website: www.TrilogyLight.com

Here is a super easy technique to
Teach yourself or anyone to
draw in one hour.

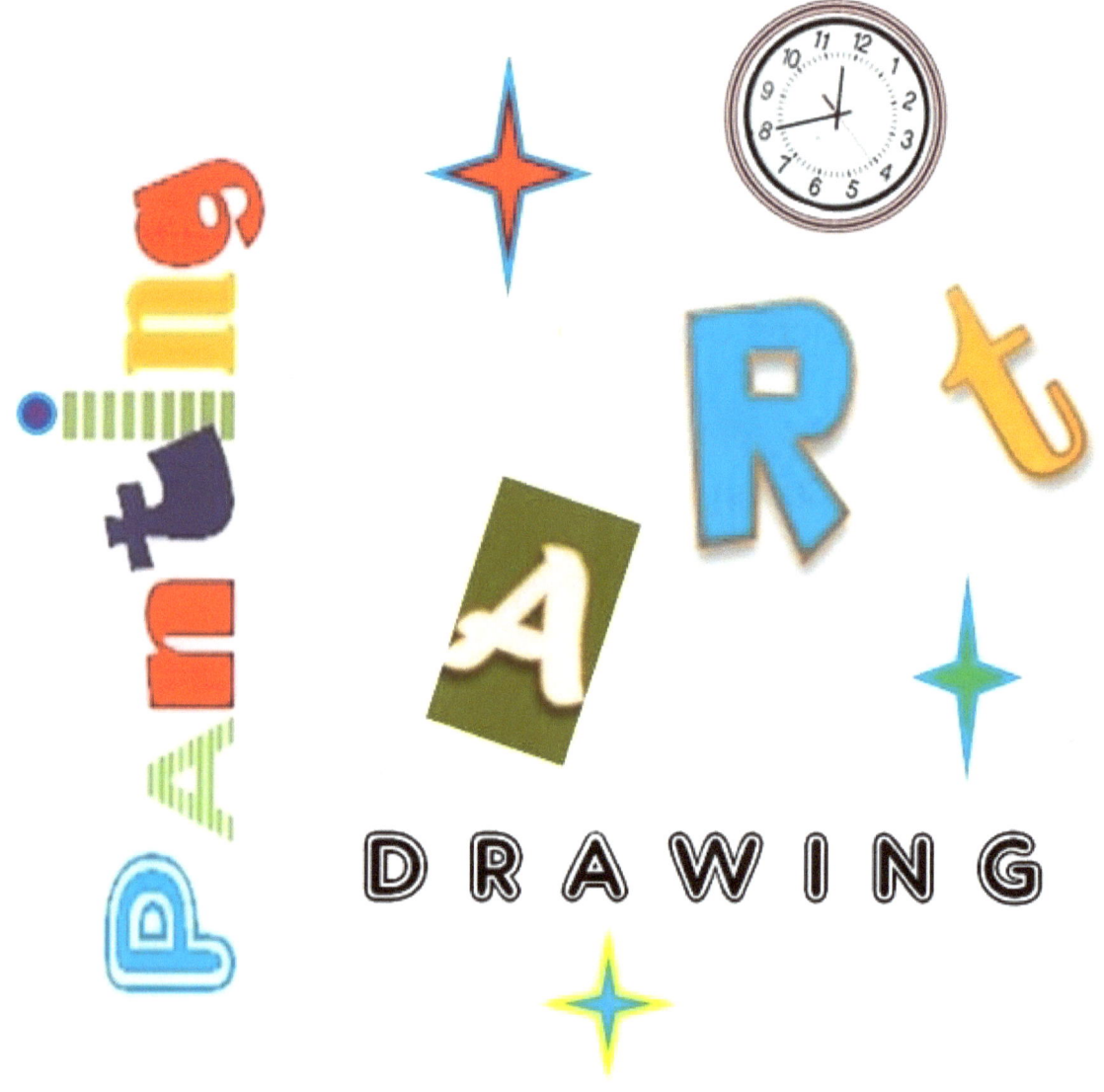

Table of Contents

INTRODUCTION

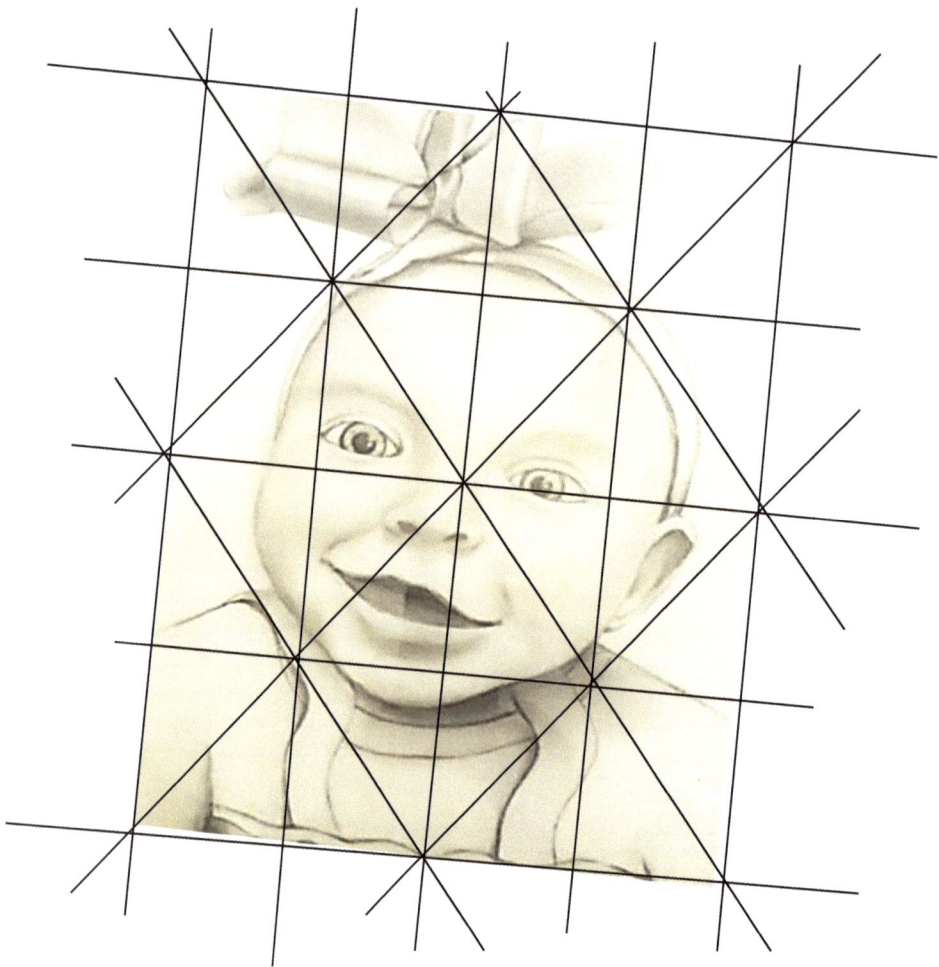

Welcome and a super thank you for getting this book that will teach you to teach other how to draw within one hour. I have taught many people of all ages this great drawing technique that is simple and easy to learn and you can do the same after learning this drawing technique that I call "Guideline and Dots Drawing or GDD".

Have you ever wanted to draw landscaping, animals, people, faces, or just about anything that you can take a photo of, but you believe your art skills are atrocious or you could never possess the skills to call yourself a good artist or have the art skills needed to teach your kids and other to draw?

Let me tell you if you can hold a ruler in your hand and make a dot then you can become a top artist. There are many kinds of drawing techniques that are taught by all kinds of artists, but the drawing technique you will learn here has been around for hundreds of years and it has been taught by many of the world's top art schools, but with the passing of decades it has become a forgotten technique.

Note; you can see that the title of the book says "Teach Anyone to Draw in One Hour". This book allows you to teach the GDD technique to those that are able to learn within about an hour; however it is about seven times easier to teach this drawing technique face-to-face to others than to teach others the same technique with this book. The reason for taking longer with the book, is that this book would require those wanting to learn the GDD technique to read the teachings, the instructions, and do the step-by-steps in order to start drawing using the GDD drawing technique. So, it may take you a bit more time to understand this GDD technique base on your reading skills, your understanding and comprehending levels, and time that you are able to devote to this book. But, once you have learned the GDD technique you should be able to teach GDD to those who are able to learn within about an hour.

Book #1 Faces

This is "Book #1 Faces", and in this book you will learn to draw faces from the photos you have or even from other photo sources. This book is perfect for them people that want to draw faces, but just feel they don't possess the skills. Once you learn the GDD technique drawing faces will be easy. If your seven years old or ninety-seven, you can learn to draw faces like top artist. More books may become available in this series of books that would use the similar technique to draw landscaping's, animals, still life, and all kinds of drawings.

Short Known History

I believe this drawing technique in the last hundred years or so has started losing followers first because of better printing presses and later because of the invention of the copier. In fact at this time I personally don't know of any followers of this technique or anyone using this drawing technique except for those people that I have taught to use these techniques and are now in love with what they have learned. This drawing technique was used before the period of the printing press as a technique that would allow artists to copy artworks from other artists and was also used by artists that sketch their drawings first on paper before painting their paintings on canvas. An artist's using this drawing technique could make small detail sketches on paper and then move the drawing with ease to a larger canvas or even many canvases without losing the drawing details.

I have not found it easy in putting together an historic background on this drawing technique because most of the people that where using this drawing technique to do their artworks have pass away. These old school artists are the ones that had a better understanding of the history of this drawing technique. However, I have seen some art books publish in the very early 1900s that have talked a bit about area lines drawing techniques, but these books have been very vague and gave very limited details on how-to teach others how to use these lines. I believe there could be some good art schools with old school art masters somewhere out there that still may be teaching these line technique, but because many of today's top art school are looking for new ideas it is possible this drawing technique may be consider antiquated for them. If this has been the case then this drawing technique has been a great loss to new artists around the world.

The historic history I was able to gather on this technique came from my memories I obtain from talking with old school artists that attended top art schools in Europe in the 50s or even going back to the 20's. In the early 1970s I had the pleasure of knowing some of these artists that where taught these techniques. One of these artists I knew was a late family member that had study back in the early 50s at a top Spanish art school and the other artists were artists I met when I was just a kid. Other artists were older folks in their mid-70s or 80s when I met them in the mid-70s. I am sure that they may have study or learn this technique back in the early1920s. After these artists showed me a bit about this technique I never again ran into or met another artist that even knew of this technique.

Early Years of Teaching the GDD Technique

On a note; before learning this technique at around the age of six I already love art it was like I was born to draw. From the 1st grade and upwards I was always known as one of the top school artists. I was able to combine the drawing technique I will teach you here in this book with my own drawing skills and was able to develop very good drawing and painting skills at a very young age.

In one incident in the early 1970s when I was attending early elementary school my home room class teacher sent me to another classroom to meet up with a teacher I have met once or twice before. When I arrived at the classroom I notice that there were no other students in the classroom and it was only her and me. She told me she had a special project for me and started to remind me of an earlier occasion when I met with her in her classroom for some studies, she then remind me that she given me some time-off at the end of the studies that I used up to do some drawings.

She then told me she was totally intrigue by a method and technique that I was using to make a drawing that day in her classroom. After reminding me of that she then inform me that my special project was to make a small book that could teach her and her kids how to draw using this drawing technique that was intriguing to her because she never seen anything like it before. I was super happy to make this small book for her that was made up of steps to make a drawing using the drawing technique I have learn from these old school artists. The book was only about five or seven pages long and she was most of the time with me as I made the book out of white lose paper sheets. It was only later in life that I believe she had called me to this empty classroom to teach her how to do this drawing technique, so it was really her that wanted to learn the technique.

In my years attending school and school art classes I never had any teacher even talk about or less teach this drawing technique at any level. From my research into this drawing technique I have found something called "line drawing", but it still nothing like this GDD technique that I will teach you here.

I have put together this book in order to teach people of young ages to adult and at all art levels how to draw anything using this forgotten drawing technique. These drawing techniques you will learn here will hopefully make you a better artist and will allow you to use these techniques not only for drawing, but you should also be able to use the GDD as a guidelines on your painting's.

Also note that I have added my own improvement to the techniques to make it easier for beginners to learn how to use and utilize the technique.

"I am sure you will not forget the GDD technique and your

level of drawing skills will become better".

Mistakes Part One

In this book drawing I have made some drawing mistakes, but I allow them in order to show you how to fix them. I don't edit out these mistakes and there is a reason why. On the last page of this book I will elaborate why I have left the mistakes within the drawing and how mistakes can help you become a better artist.

Before You Start

**Before you start here are the items you would
need to have in order to get started**

1. You would need a pencil or pencil set. (It's best to have an artist pencil set).

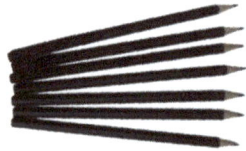

2. Pencil Sharpener.

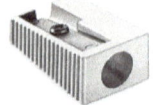

3. Pencil Eraser.

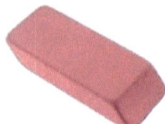

4. Fine Drawing Paper.

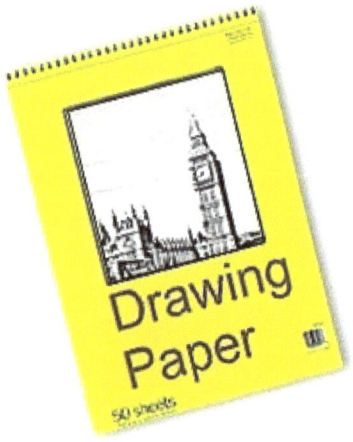

5. Drawing Ruler, best to have a transparent ruler.

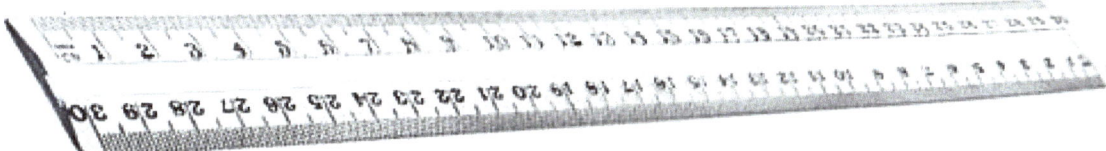

Optional items you may want for drawing.

A Cake Board that is bigger than the drawing paper you'll be using. In my years of drawing I found that cake boards make very good surface for doing artwork using pencil. I believe its way better to use a cake board then a book or magazine. Also, you'll need some wrapping tape about inch and-half and it's not a good idea to use a thin wrapping tape, because you may end up tearing your corners.

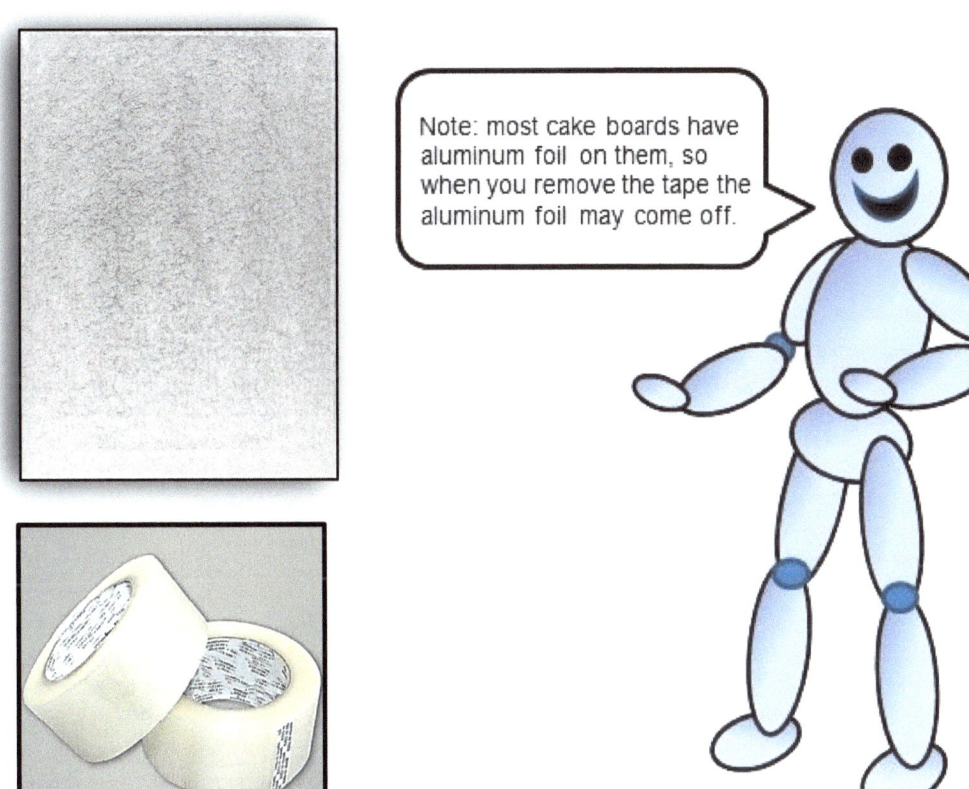

How to prepare your board, so you can start drawing.

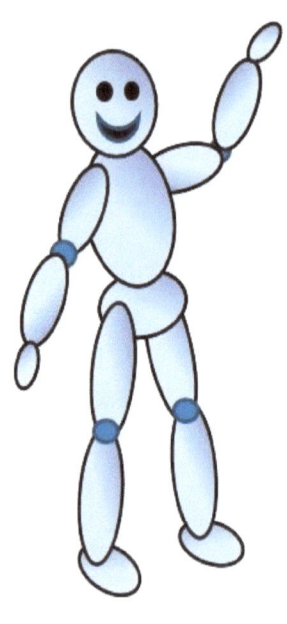

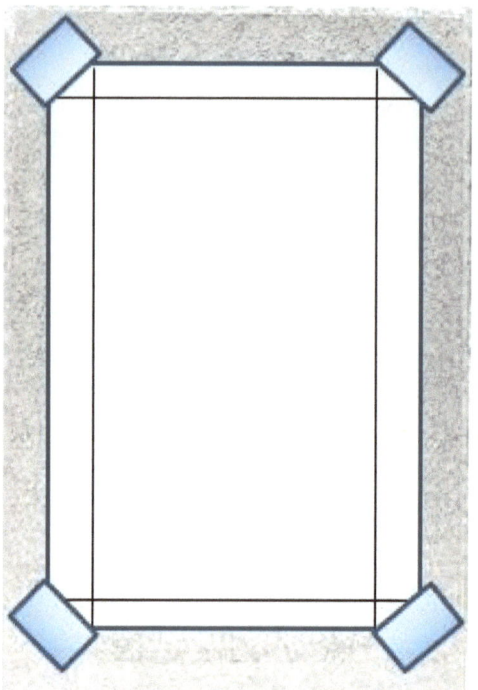

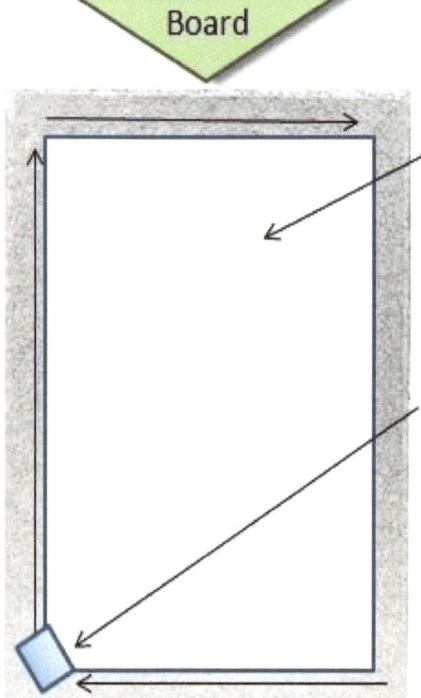

Board

Step 1, lay down your art paper on your board and make sure your board is wider than your paper by an inch or a inch and a-half more than your art paper.

Step 2, add tape to each corner of the paper and make sure your tape is about an inch wide to inch and a half wide. A wider tape may help to prevent the corner of the paper tearing away when you're drawing.

Once you have completed step 1 and 2 you have two options. One you can leave the board like option one or the second option; you can add borders to your drawing paper. The borders are added in case your paper tears when your drawing on it or it tears when you remove the tape from the corners.

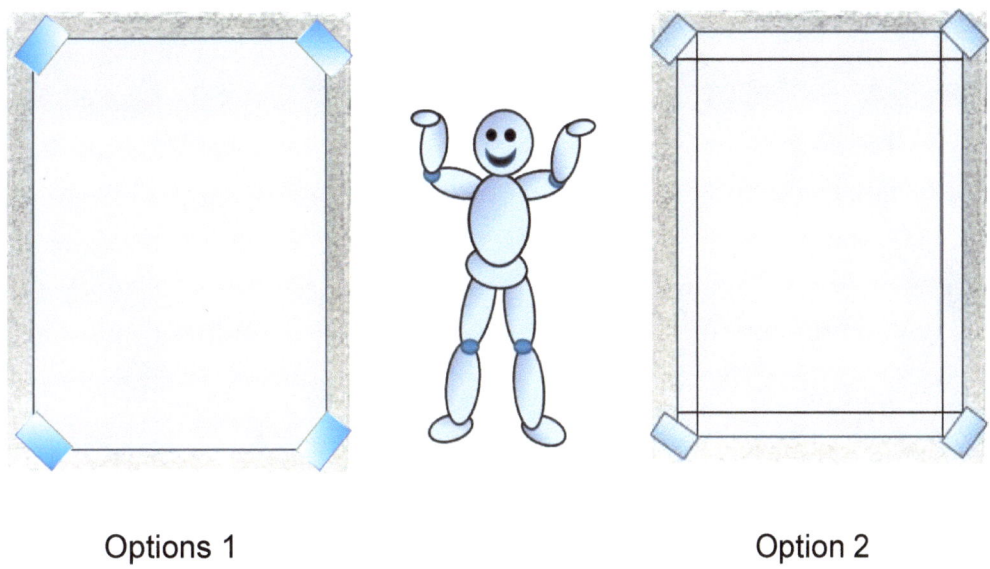

Options 1   Option 2

If you like to applied borders and your drawing paper is big enough you can use the thickness of the ruler as a guideline.

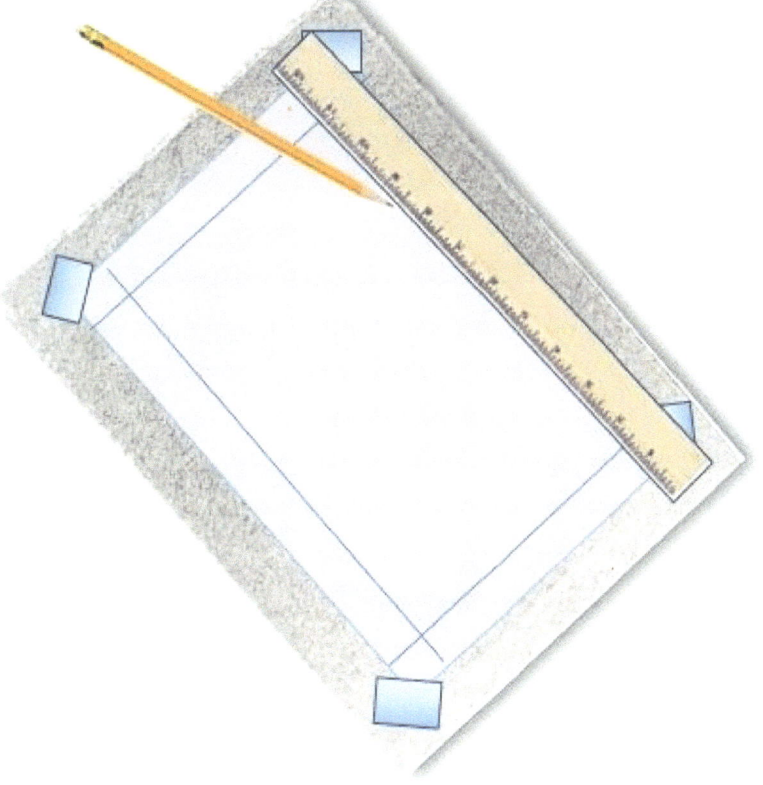

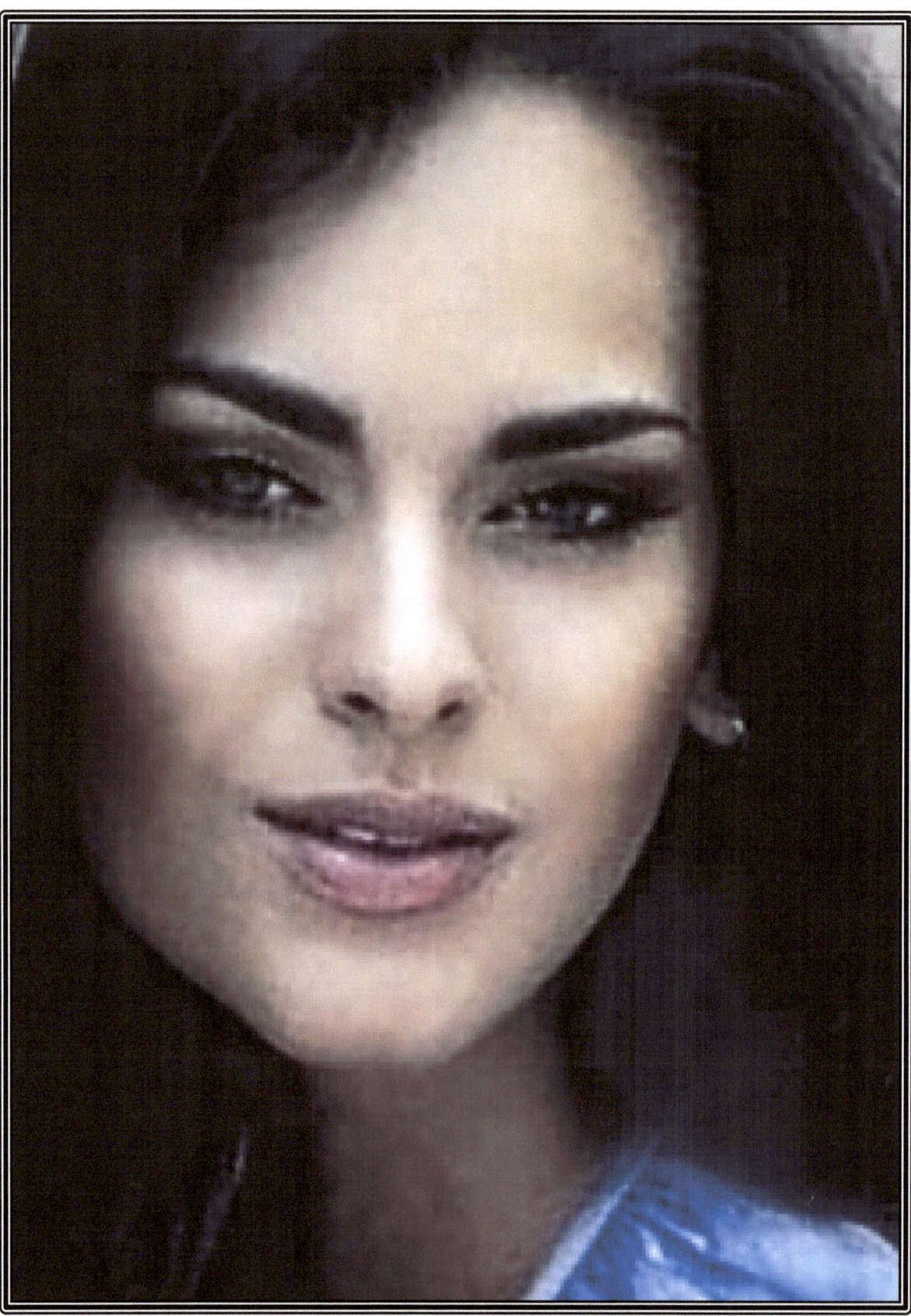

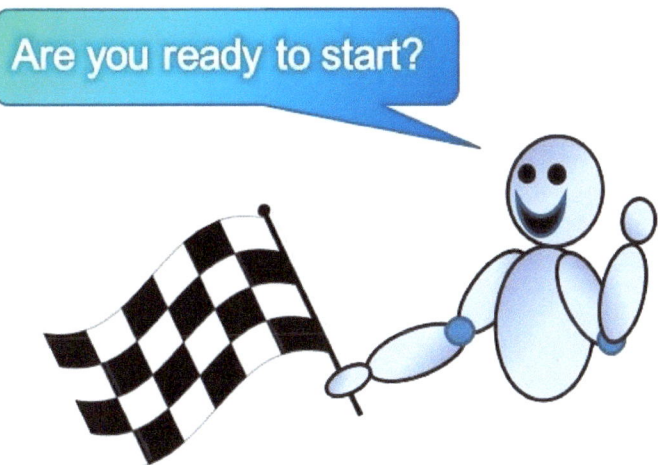

Some more notes before we get started, on the previous page there is a photo with a lady's face that we will use to do our drawing. However, it is not necessary to use this photo in this book for your lessons. If you would like to use your own photos this would be just fine, but make sure you're using a person's face photo for this lesson.

We will be using this photo of the lady, so if you're not using your own photo and you're going to use this one then you'll be require to photocopy it, because you'll be drawing on the photo and I am sure you don't want to ruined the book by removing the photo. If you're going to use your own photos and you don't want to ruin them then you're going to have to copy them.

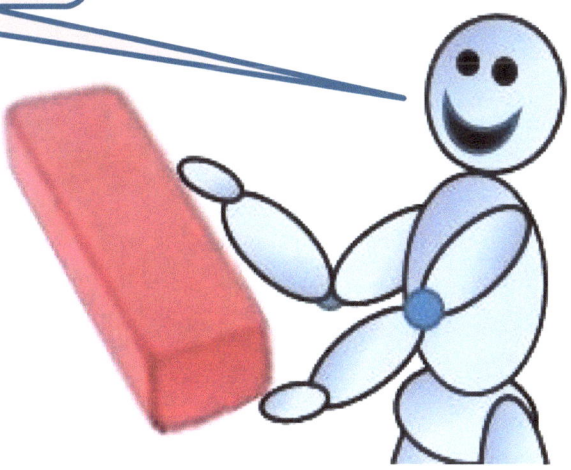

Lesson 1.0 Beginners Level

On this lesson you would need the face photo, your pencil, and your ruler.

Step 1.0, take your photo and place it in the area you going to work on. We will now start drawing are guidelines. (Note my guidelines will be in yellow, so you can see them better and also note you will be drawing on your photo or the copy of your photo.)

Using your ruler make a line from the top lift corner to the right bottom corner. Next draw a line from the right top corner to the bottom lift corner. Next you will draw a line from the middle of the top of your photo to the middle of the bottom of your photo. Next draw a line from the middle of the lift side to the middle right side. Now, keep drawing lines on your photo as you see them on the photo I am placing the guidelines on.

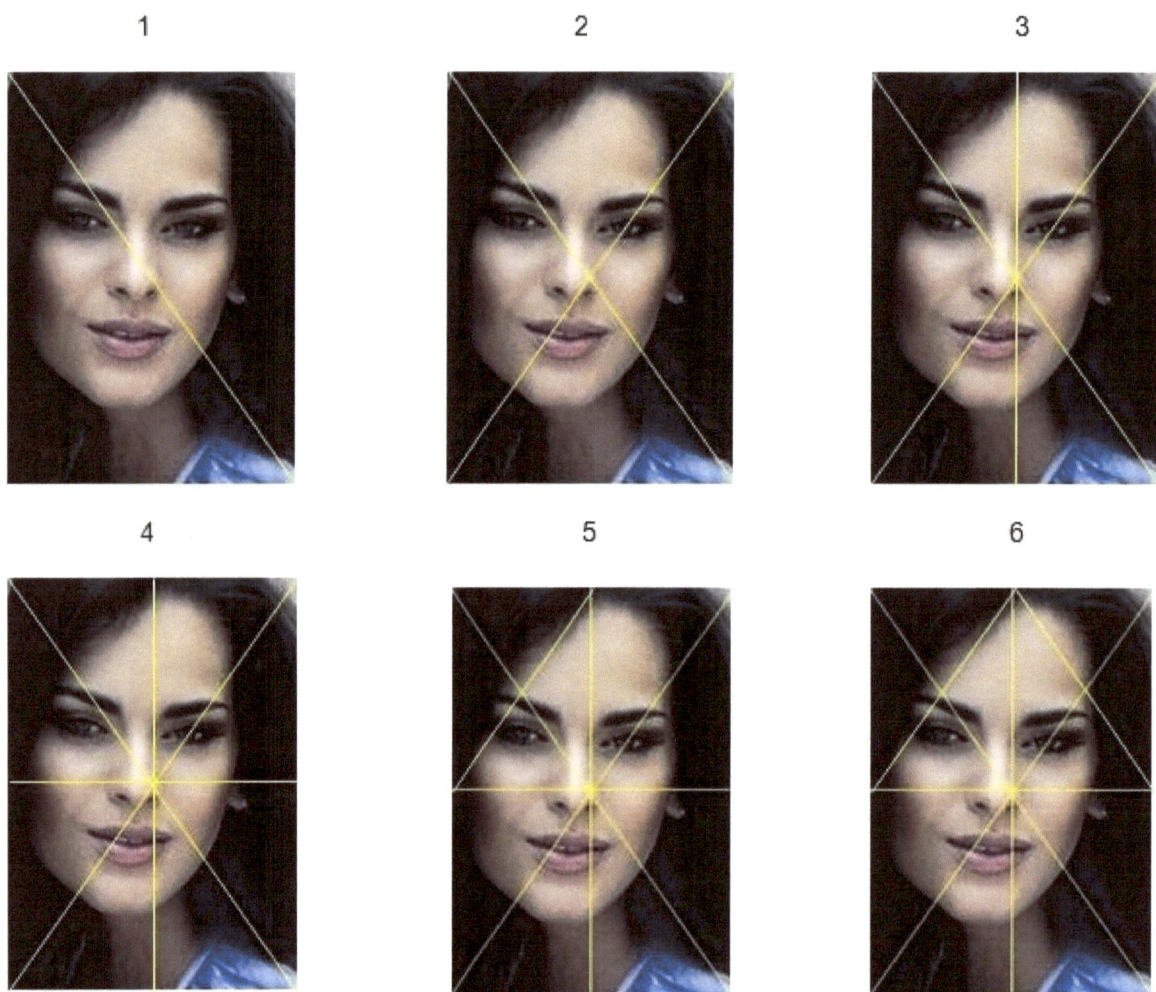

7   8 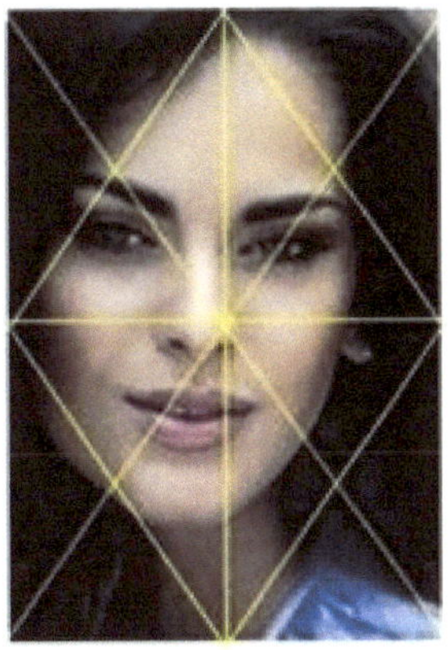   9

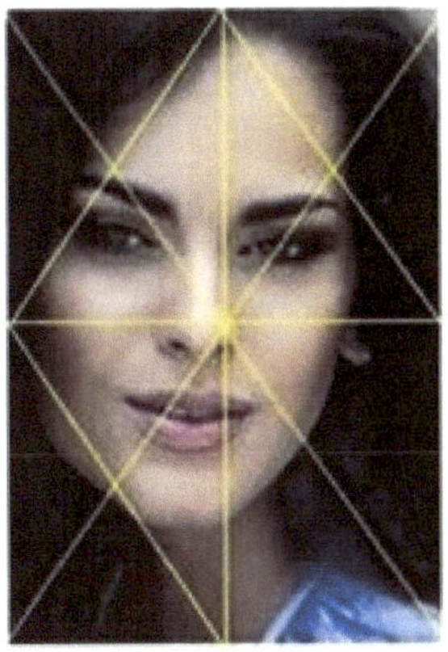

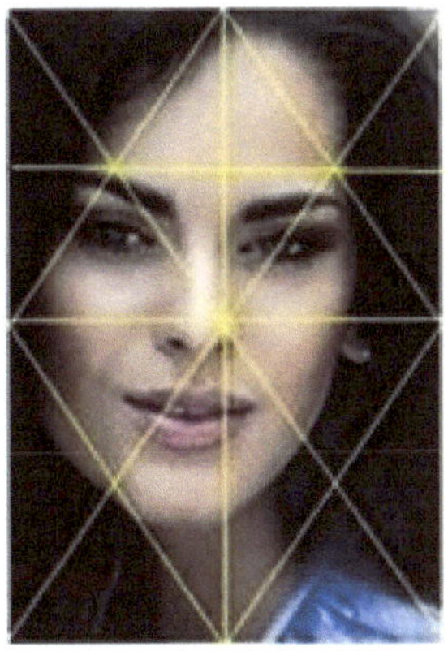

10 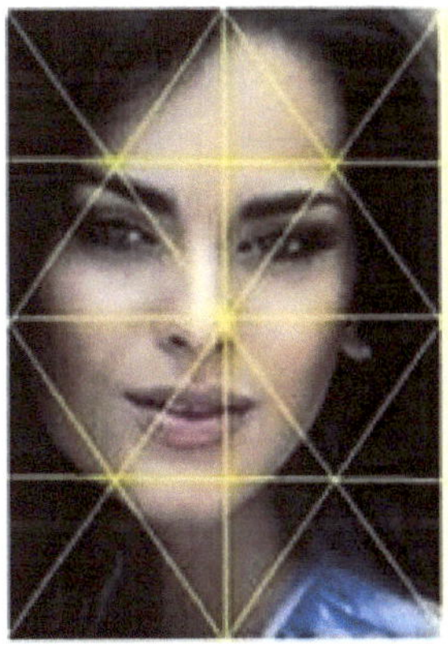   11 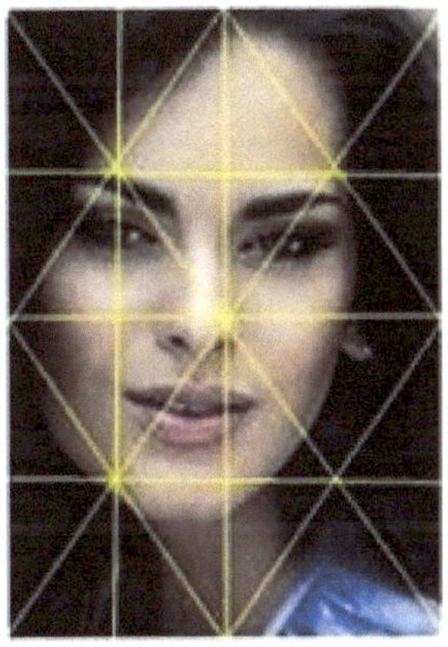   12

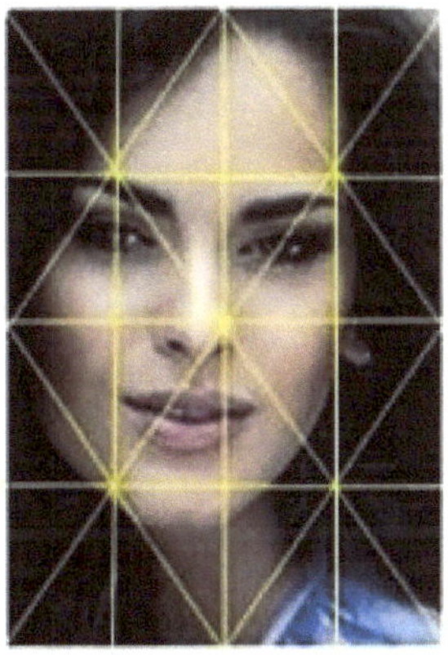

This is how your photo should look like with the guidelines. If your photo has all the line and all the lines are in the right places then you are done with step 1.

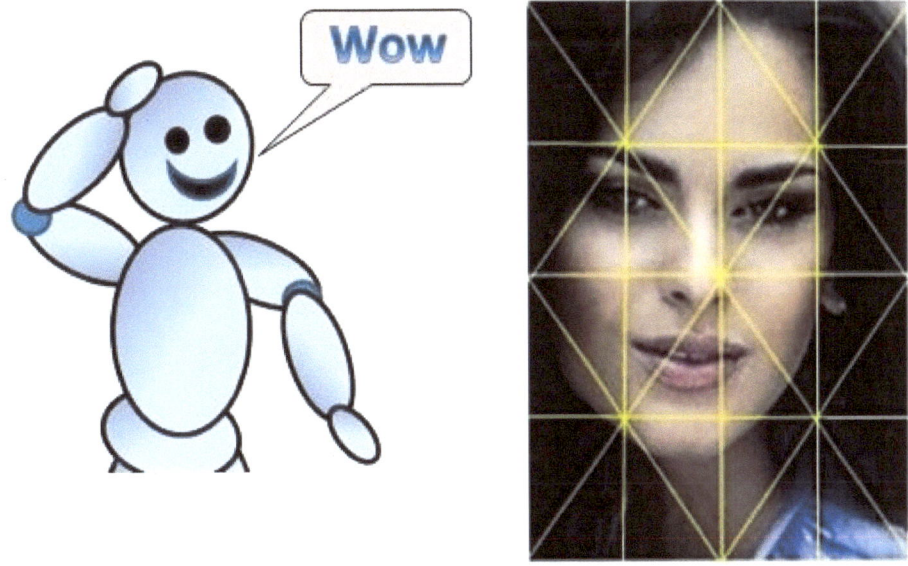

Lesson 1.0 Beginners Level

Step 2.0, in this step you will be doing the same lines on the paper you're going to be doing your drawing. (Note: I am going to be doing the lines on the art paper without the borders.) When you make the lines on your paper try making the line very lite.

Using your ruler make a line from the top lift corner to the right bottom corner. Next draw a line from the right top corner to the bottom lift corner. Next you will draw a line from the middle of the top of your photo to the middle of the bottom of your photo. Next draw a line from the middle of the lift side to the middle right side. Now, keep drawing lines on your photo as you see them on the photo I am placing the guidelines on.

1

2

3

4

5

6

7

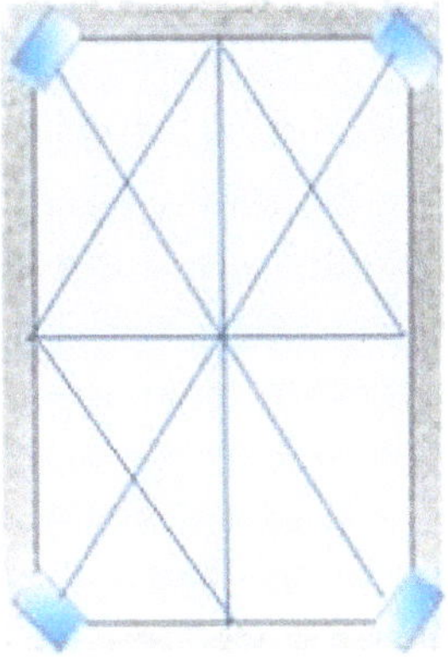

8

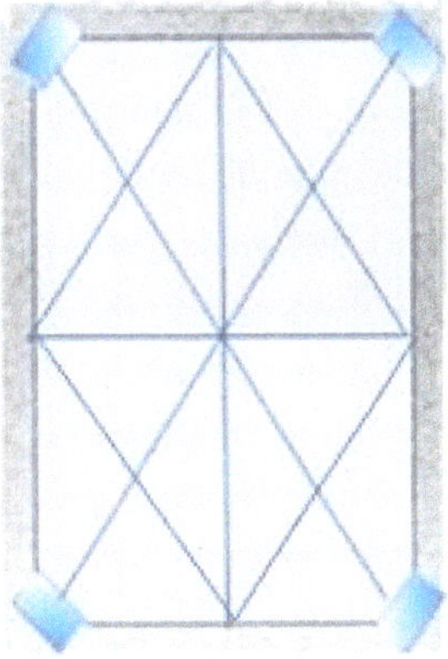

9

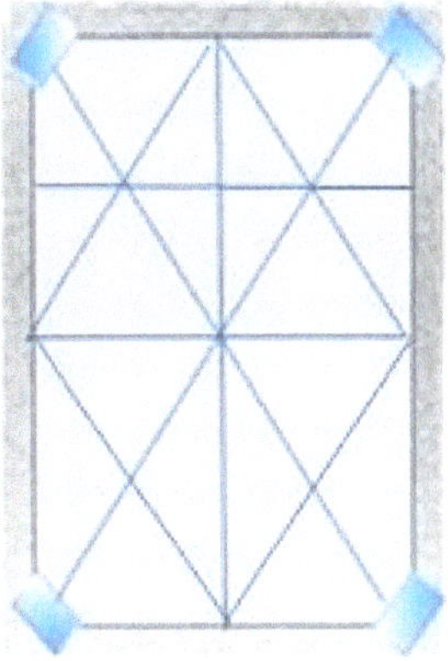

10

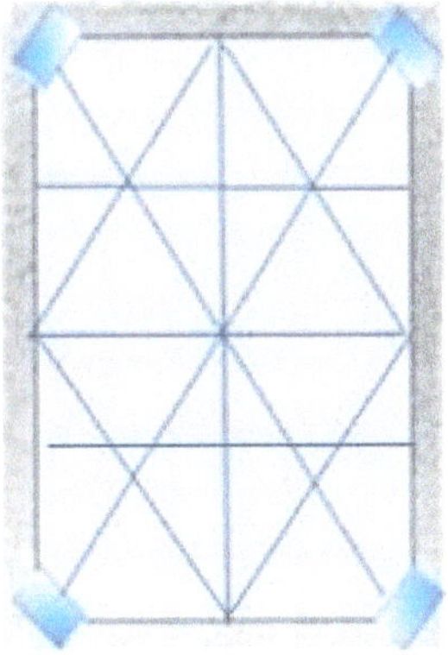

11

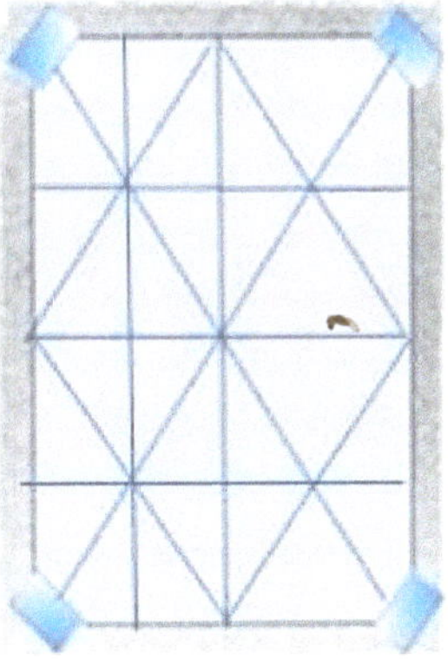

12

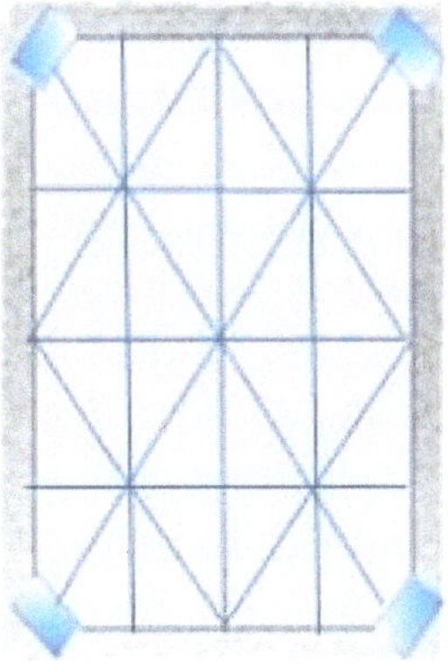

This is how your drawing paper should look like with the guidelines. If your drawing paper has all the line and all the lines are in the right place then you are done with step 2.

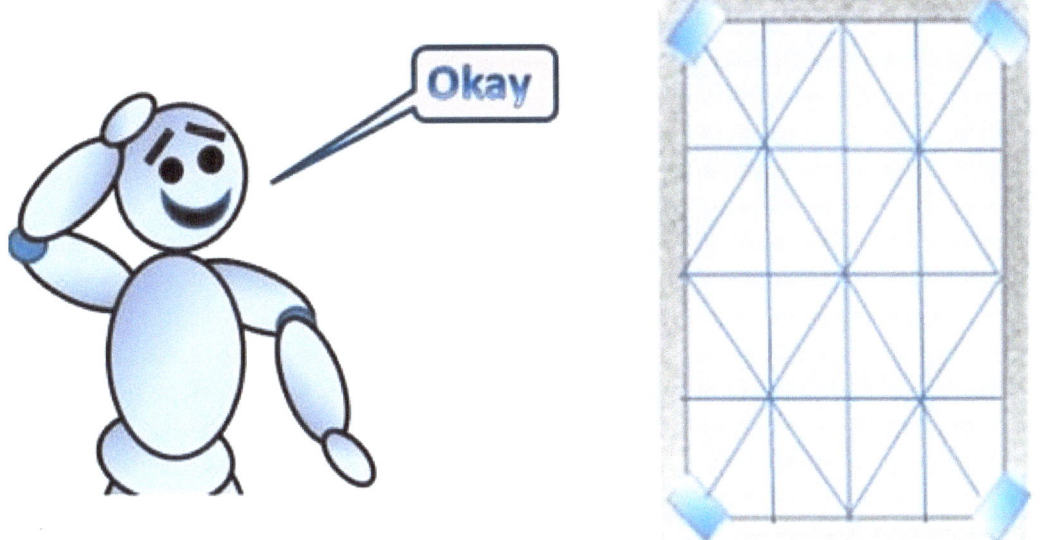

Okay

Lesson 1.0 Beginners Level

Step 3.0, because this may be your first time doing a GDD I add one more thing to your drawing paper for instructional purposes of this book then later when you do other GDDs you made not need to add this. However people may want to add this reference points to all the drawings they do, but it will add a bit more erasing work on your drawings. Add these numbers and letters as I place them on here to your drawing paper, but remember to keep them small and lite.

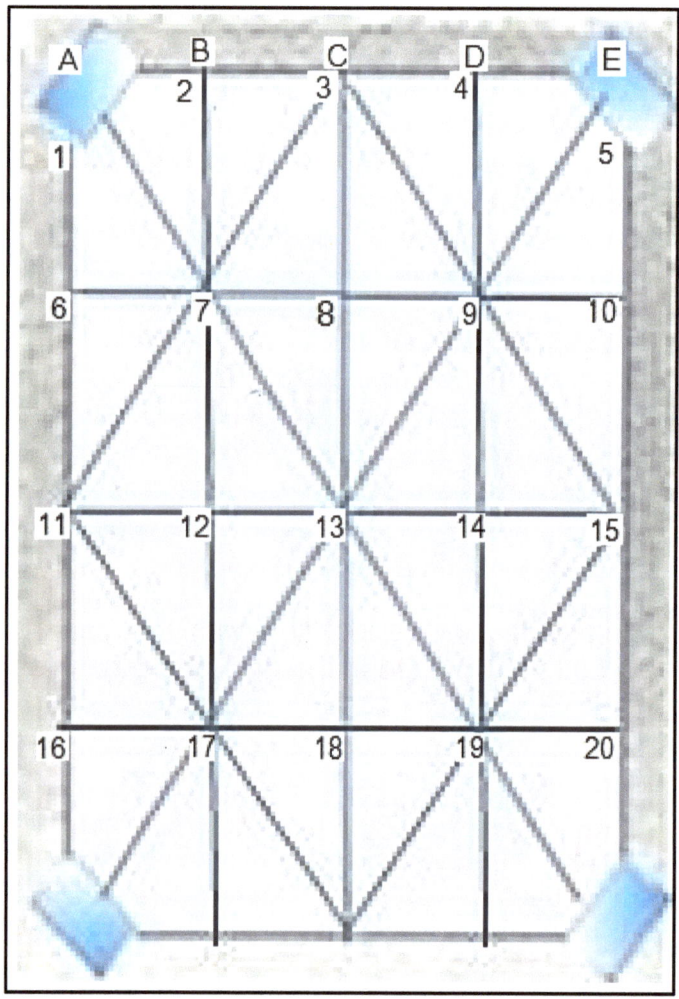

Lesson 1.0 Beginners Level

Step 4.0, we will start now doing the hands on drawing, below you'll see my art paper prepare. I have made the lines on my paper darker, so you can see how I used the guideline to do the drawing, but your lines should be a lot lighter than my. Note: as you do your drawing place the photo with the lines somewhere next to where you're doing your drawing, so you can start using the guidelines as reference for your drawing. You can add as many dots as you want and as you gain confidence in your drawing skills I am sure you'll be adding fewer dots.

We will start doing the area of the jaw that I have herein have indicated in blue.

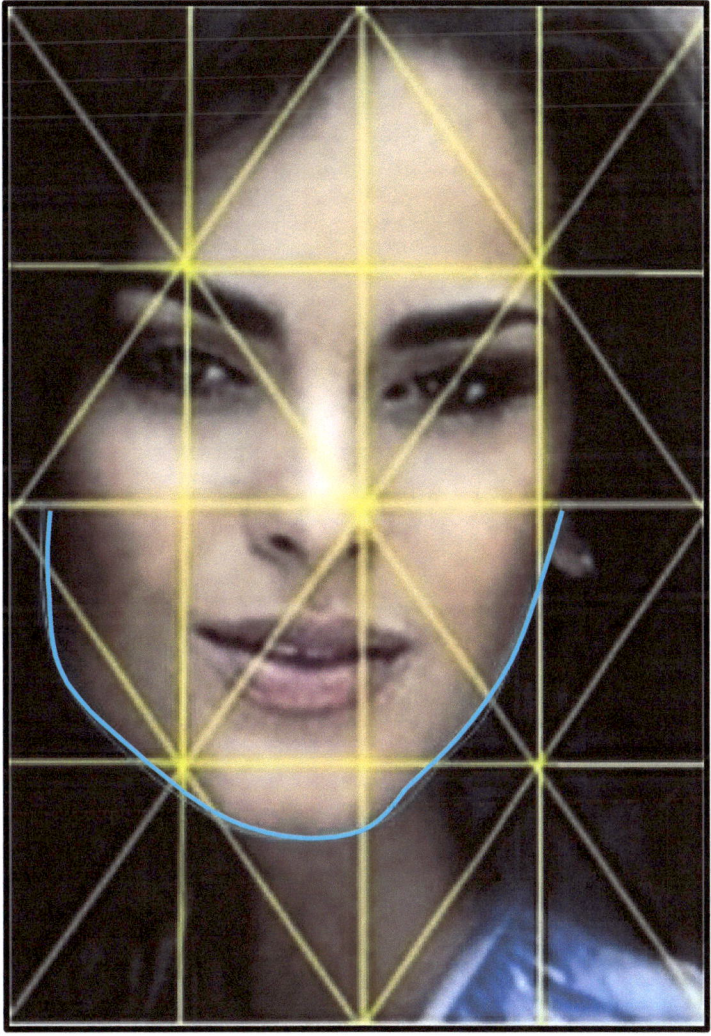

Lesson 1.0 Beginners Level

Step 5.0, we will use points or dots (●) to mark areas before drawing the lines point-to-point. Look at 11-A and put the first small dot about one 3rd of the way in from the 11 line. (Remember to keep all marks and lines lite and small) At every curve and/or corner you need to add a small dot. You'll use the jawline on the photo as your reference where to put the dots. Follow along with me and you'll begin to understand what I am doing and before you know it you'll be putting the dots on your own.

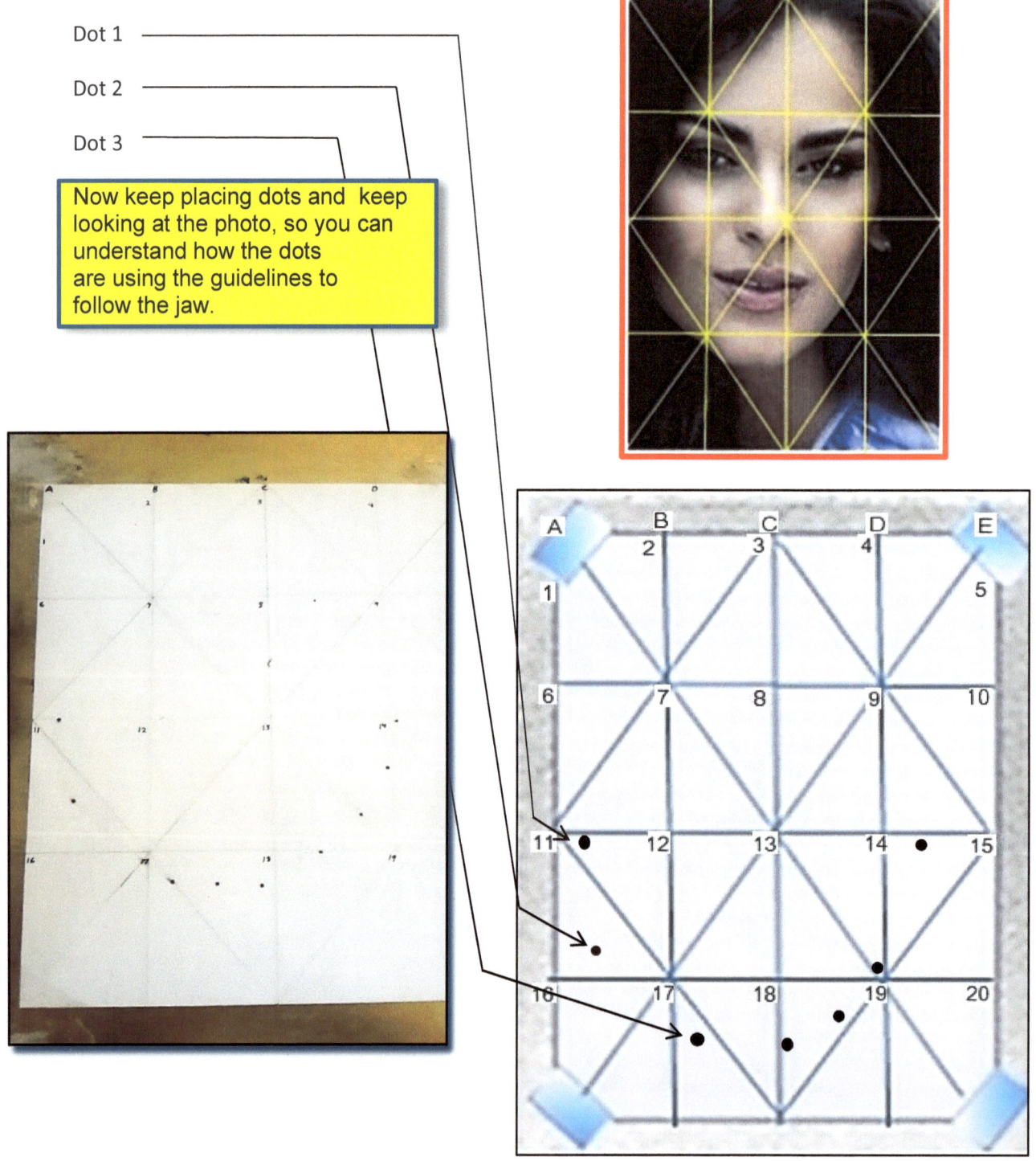

Dot 1

Dot 2

Dot 3

Now keep placing dots and keep looking at the photo, so you can understand how the dots are using the guidelines to follow the jaw.

Lesson 1.0 Beginners Level

Step 6.0, now we will connect the dots before we move on to the next steps.

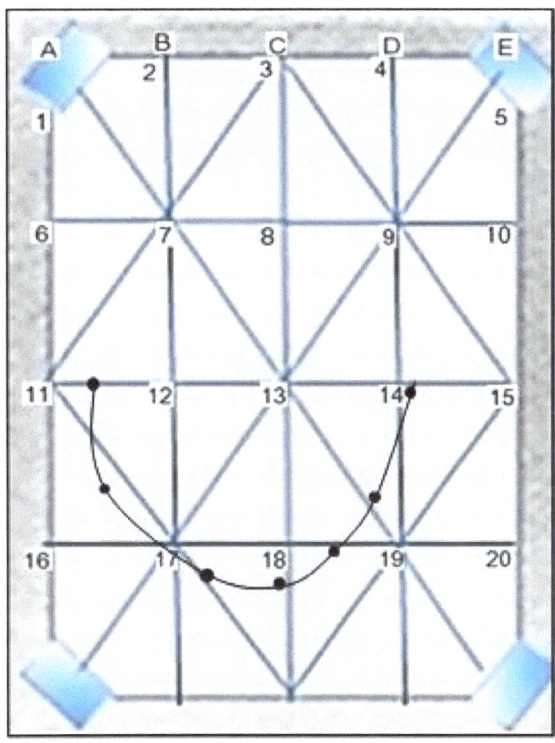

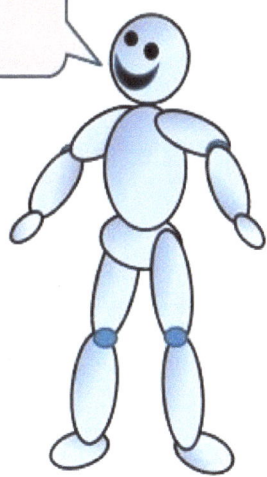

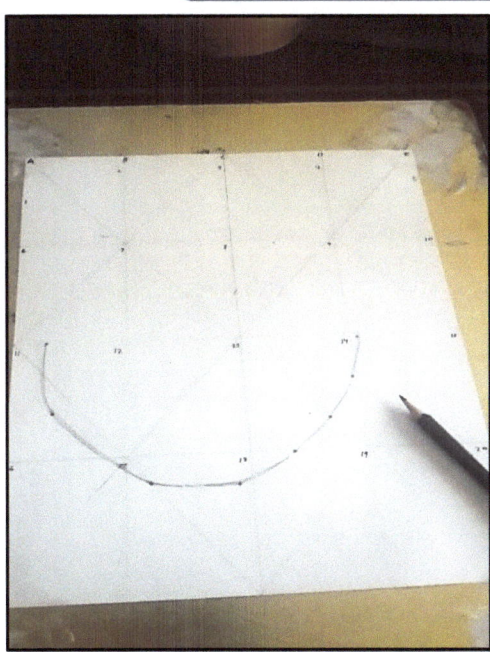

Lesson 1.0 Beginners Level

Step 7.0, we will now finish the top half of the face, so we start about a 3rd of the way in from 11-A and put the next dot almost in the middle of 6-A . Then you would put your next dot about 1/4 down from line 6-A and about 1/4 of the way in from 7-B.

Dot 1

Dot 2

Dot 3

Now keep placing the dots and keep looking at the photo, so you can understanding how the dots are using the guidelines for the upper face.

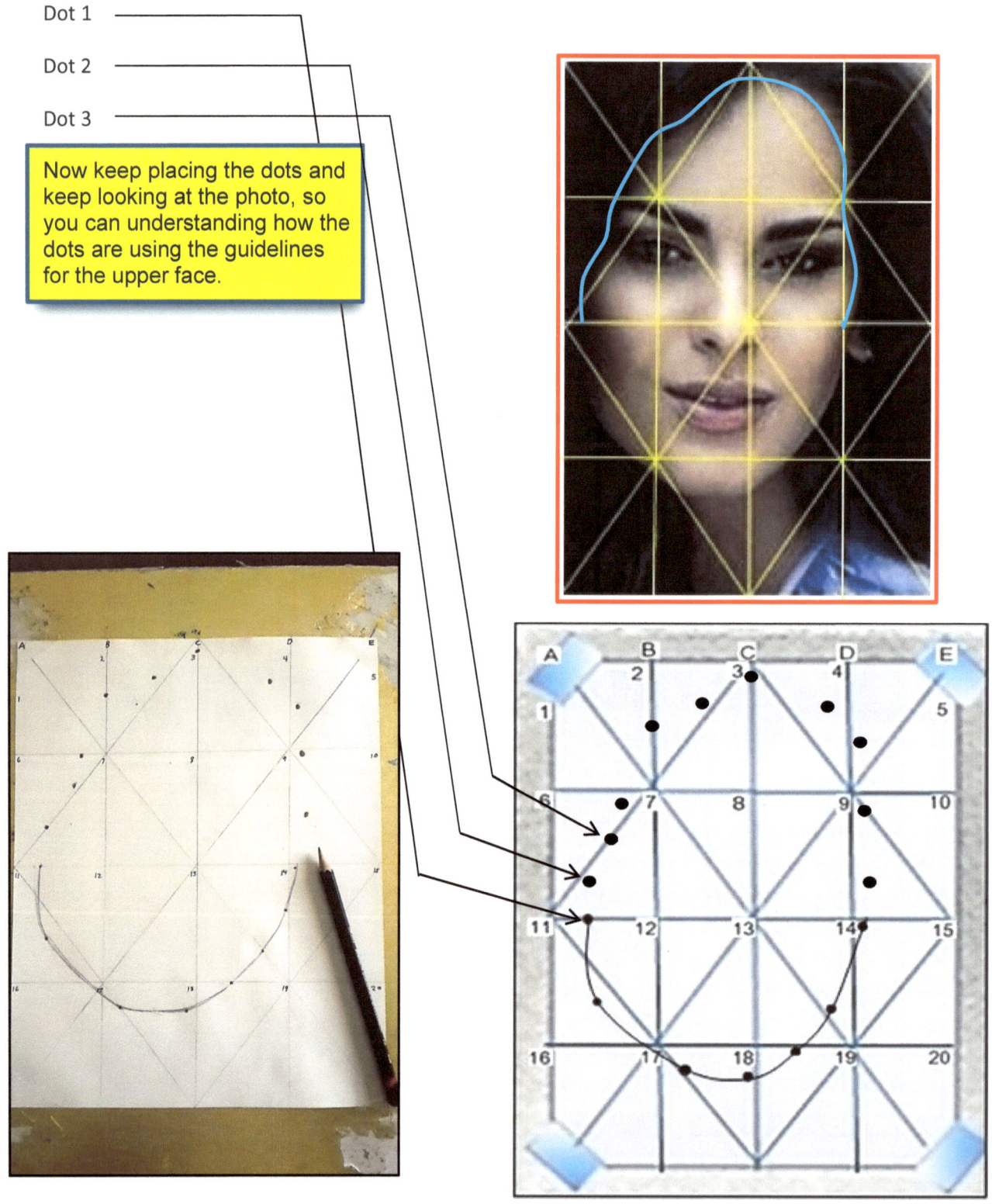

Lesson 1.0 Beginners Level

Step 8.0, now we will connect the dots before we move on to the next steps. Note; do not just make straight lines from one dot to the other. You should be looking at the contour of the face because in many cases the line will not be straight and may have a curve, so draw from one dot to the other dot according to how the line contours.

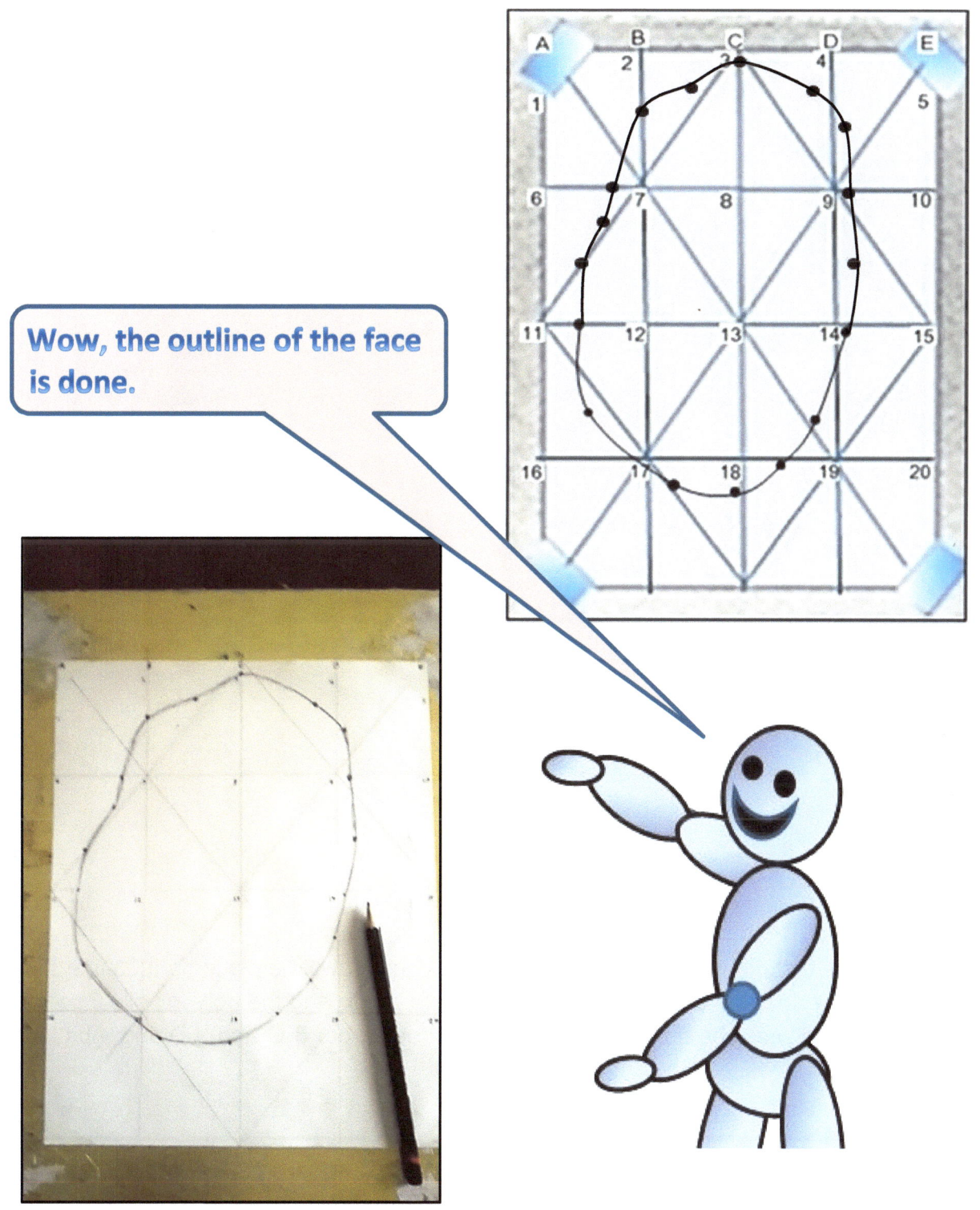

Lesson 1.0 Beginners Level

Step 9.0, in this step it will seem more difficult, but it's not just keep using the guidelines in the photo and place the dots in the right places and when you have connected the dots you'll see you have done a good job. We now start with the eyes, so to make things easier to understand I have enlarge the eyes area so you can see better in order to do this area.

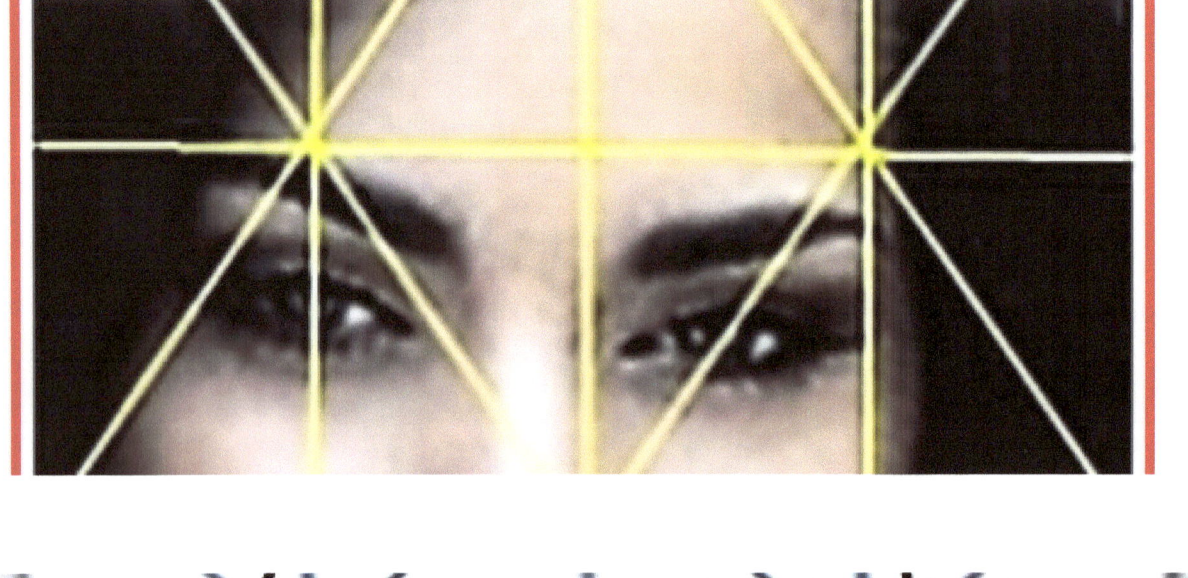

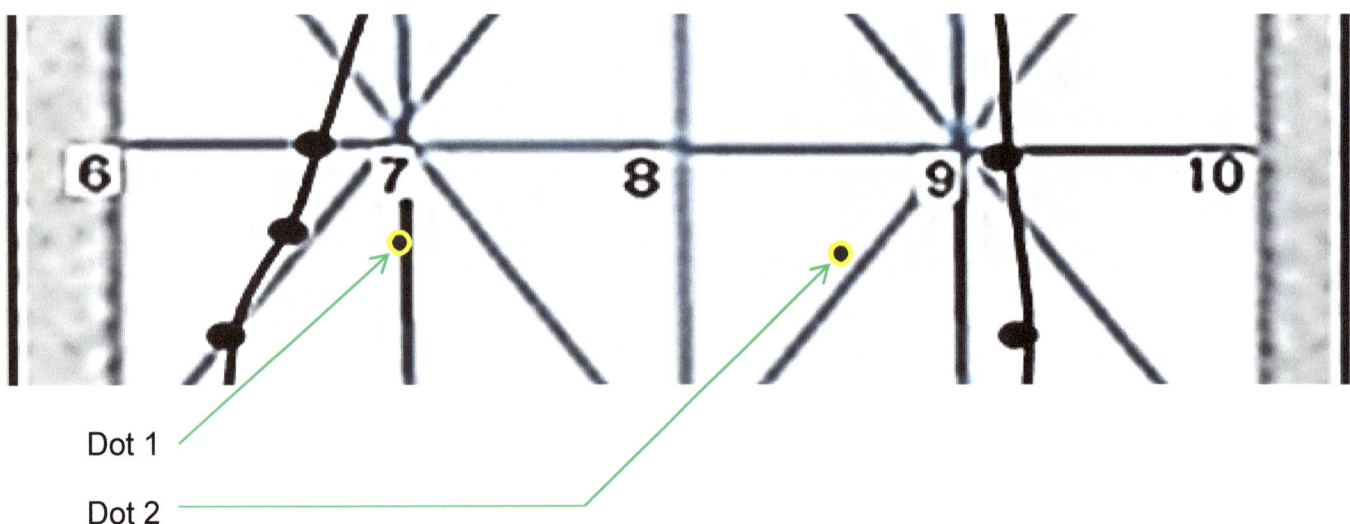

Dot 1

Dot 2

We will put the first dot where the center of the eye goes it will be place right on line 7-B almost half way down. Note; I have made the line in green and the dots in yellow so it's easier for you to see. The next center is half way down from 8-C and 9-D and a bit low then the first dot.

Lesson 1.0 Beginners Level

Now we will put the dots on the edge of her eyes.

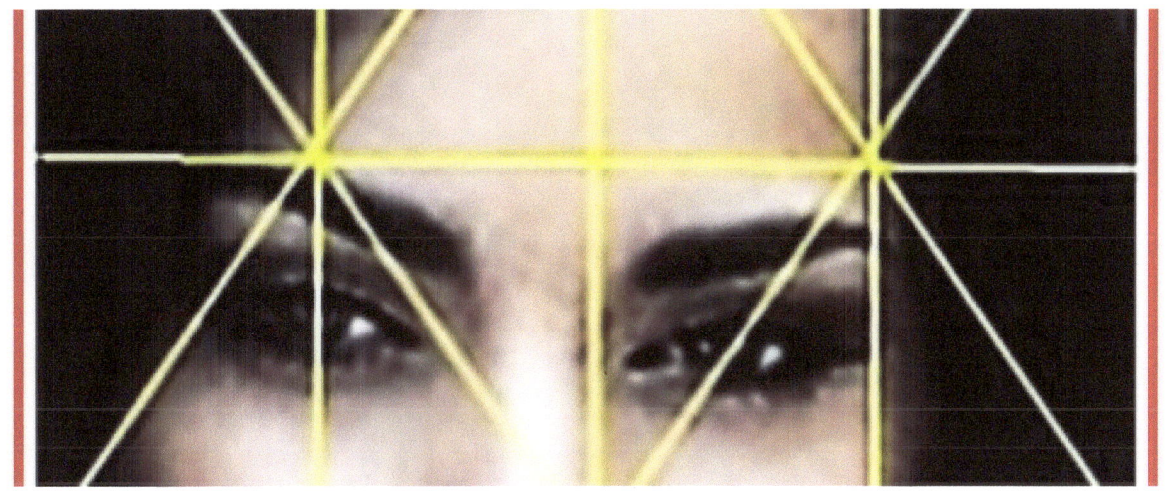

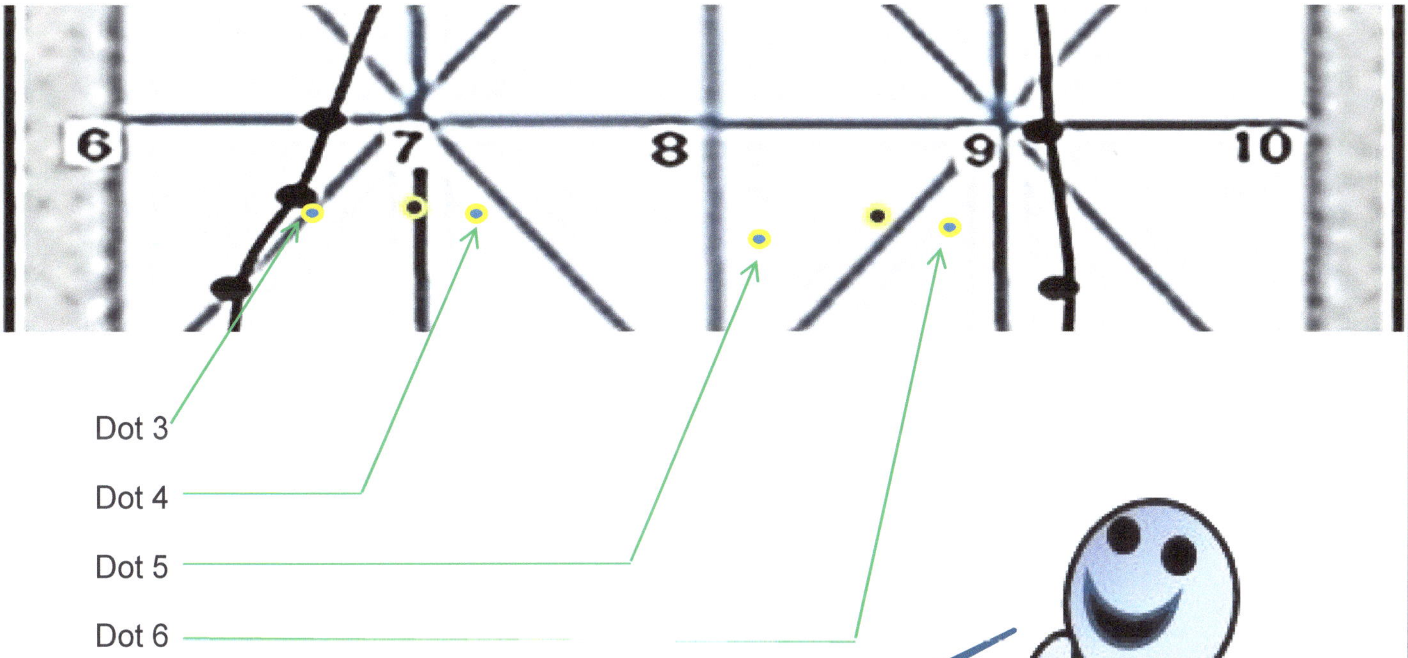

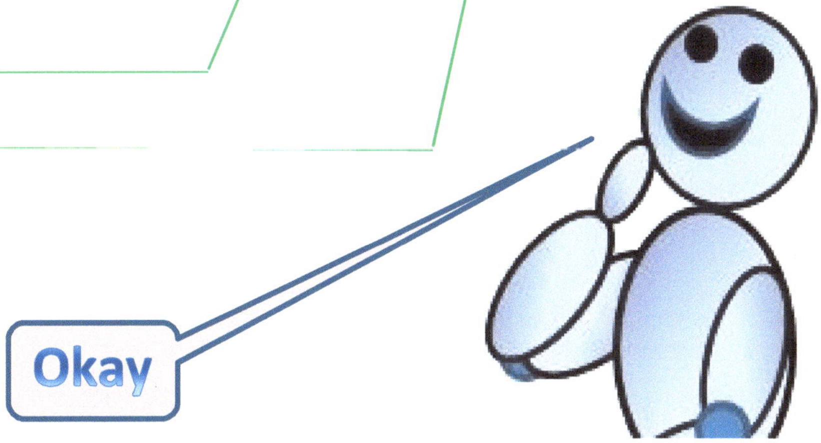

Dot 3

Dot 4

Dot 5

Dot 6

Okay

Lesson 1.0 Beginners Level

Now we will finish off the dots in the eyes.

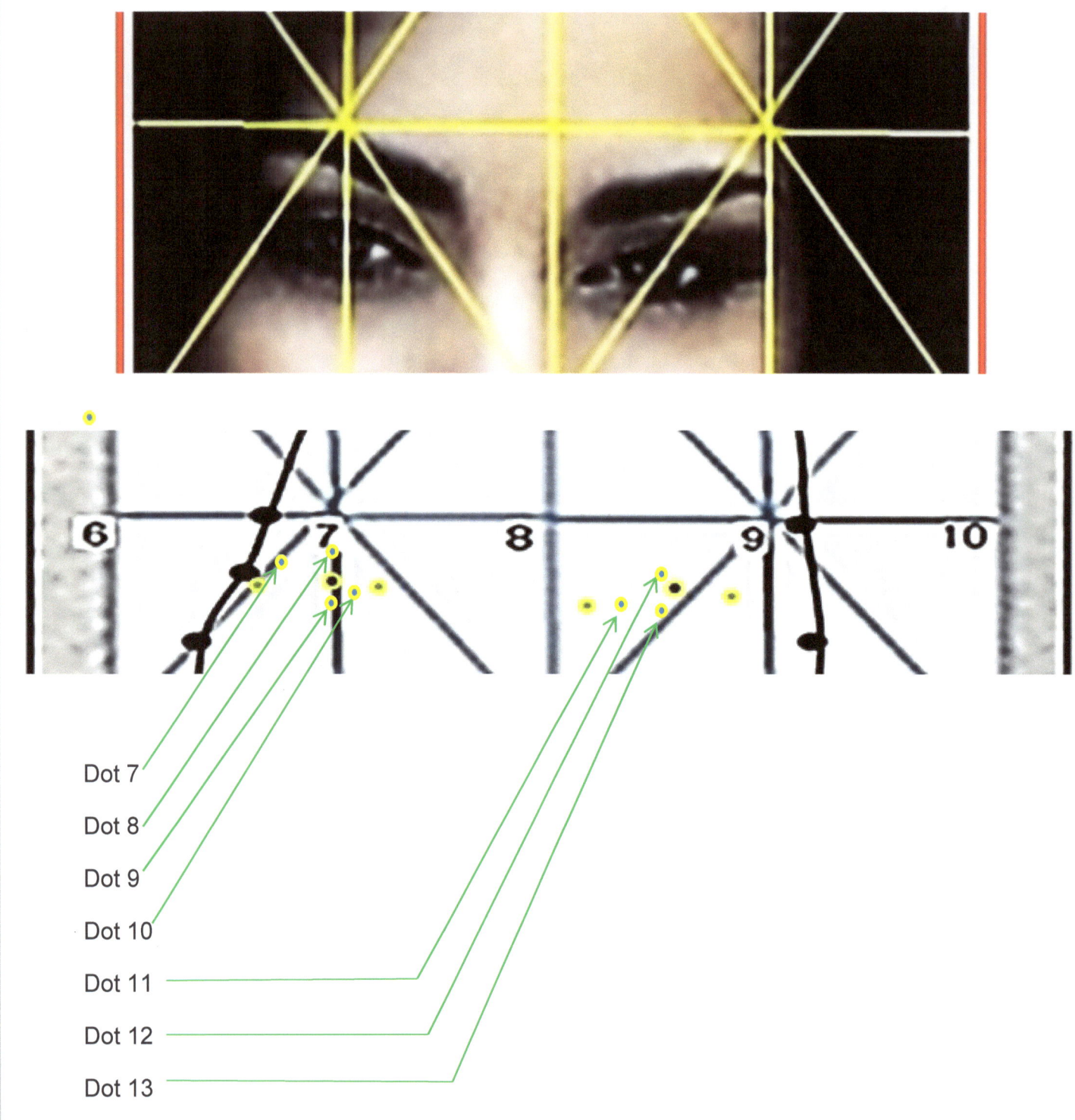

Dot 7

Dot 8

Dot 9

Dot 10

Dot 11

Dot 12

Dot 13

Lesson 1.0 Beginners Level

Step 10.0, we will now connect the dots, but do not connect the center eyeball dots with anything.

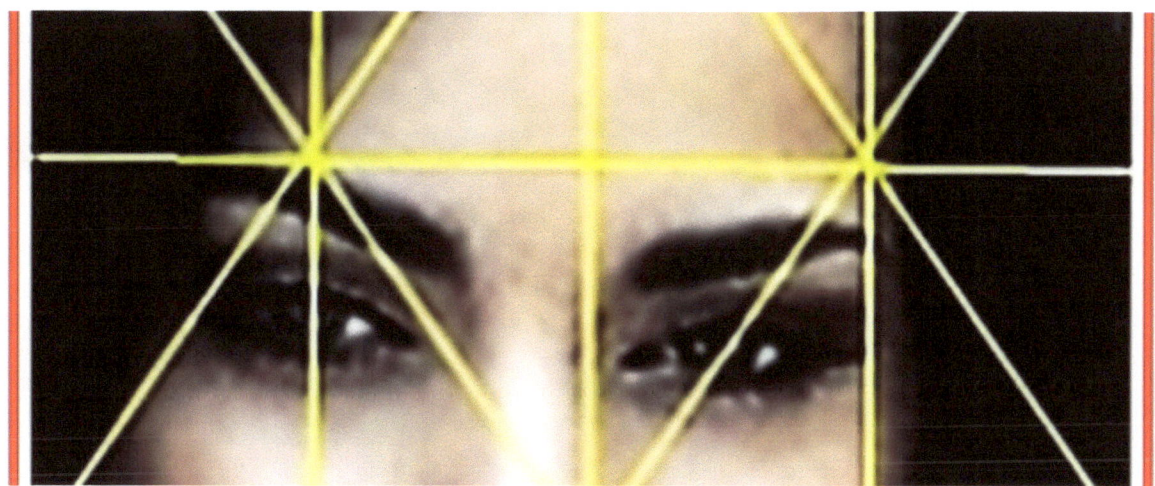

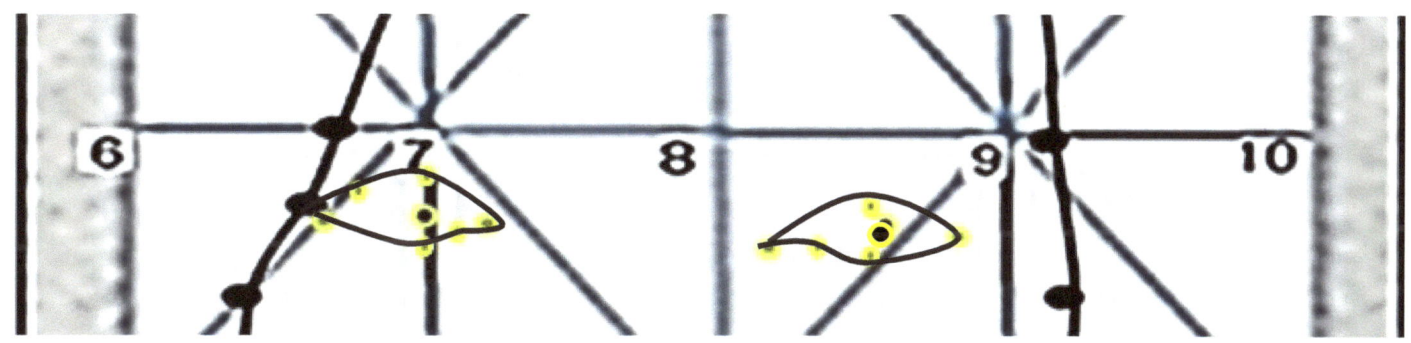

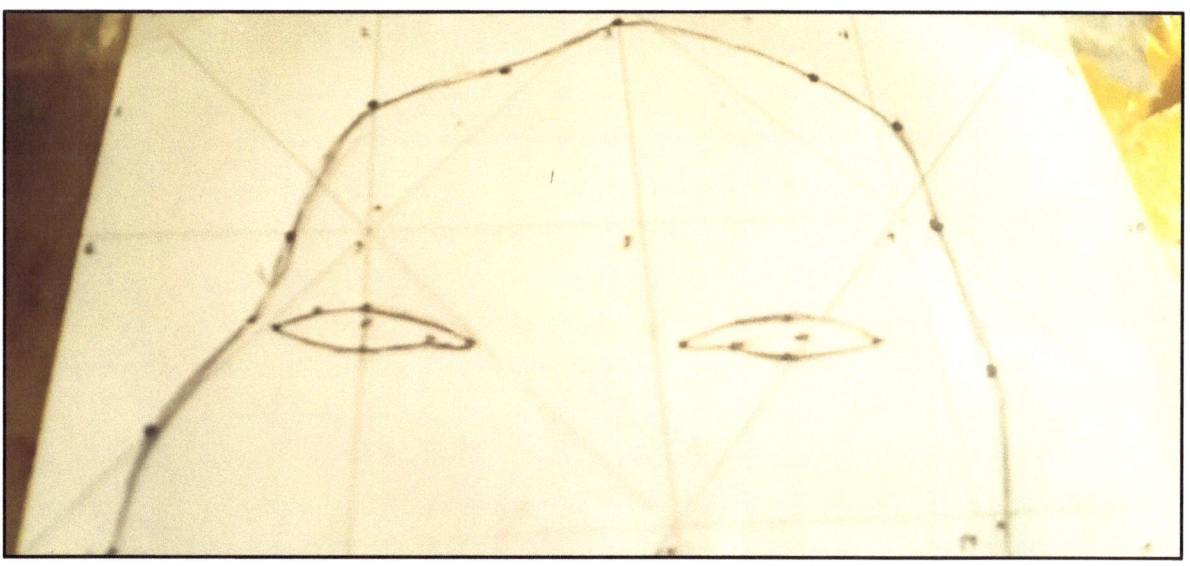

Lesson 1.0 Beginners Level

Step 11.0, the next step will be to make the eyebrows.

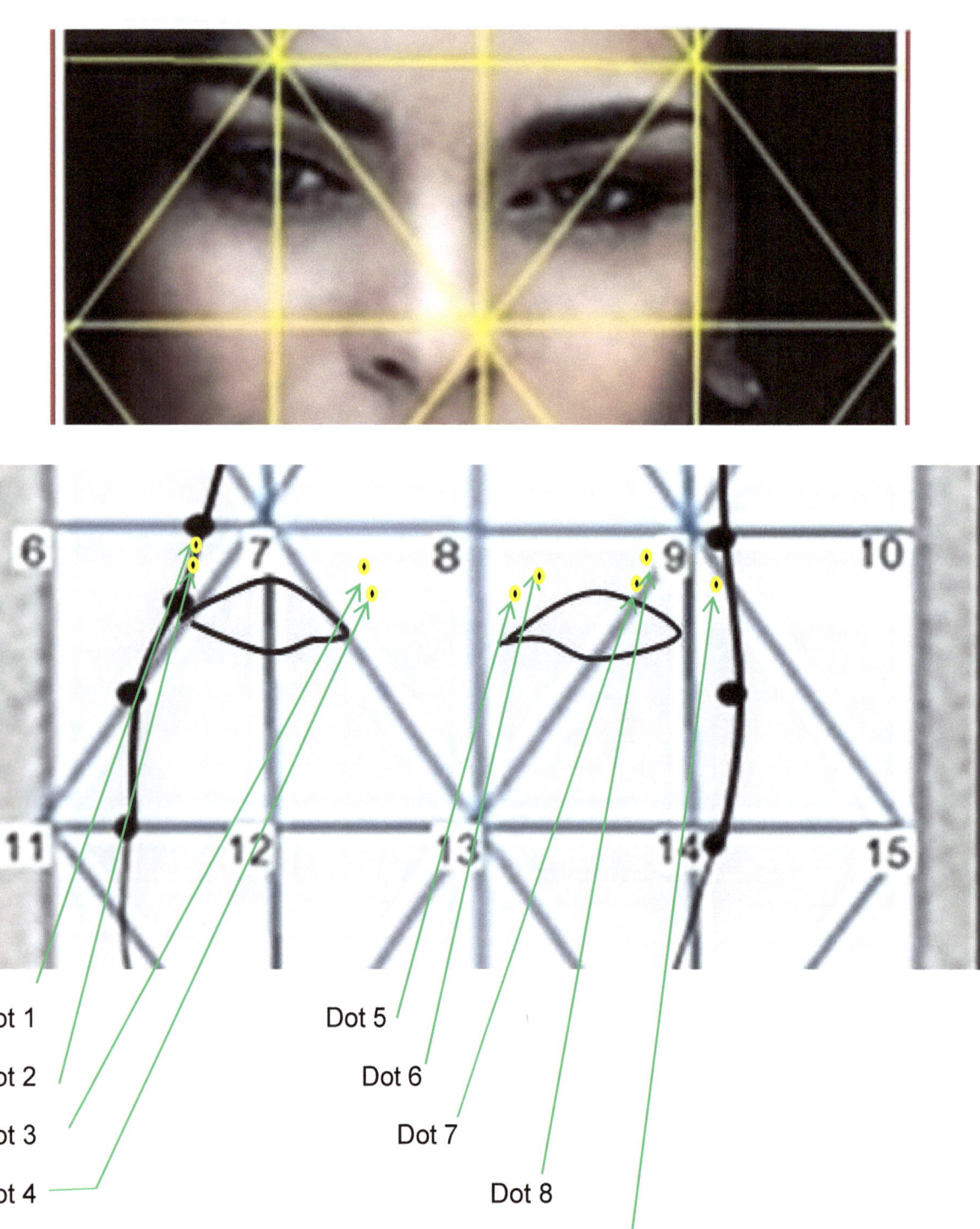

Dot 1

Dot 2

Dot 3

Dot 4

Dot 5

Dot 6

Dot 7

Dot 8

Dot 9

Lesson 1.0 Beginners Level

Step 12.0, now connect the dots of the first eyebrow and then the next eyebrow.

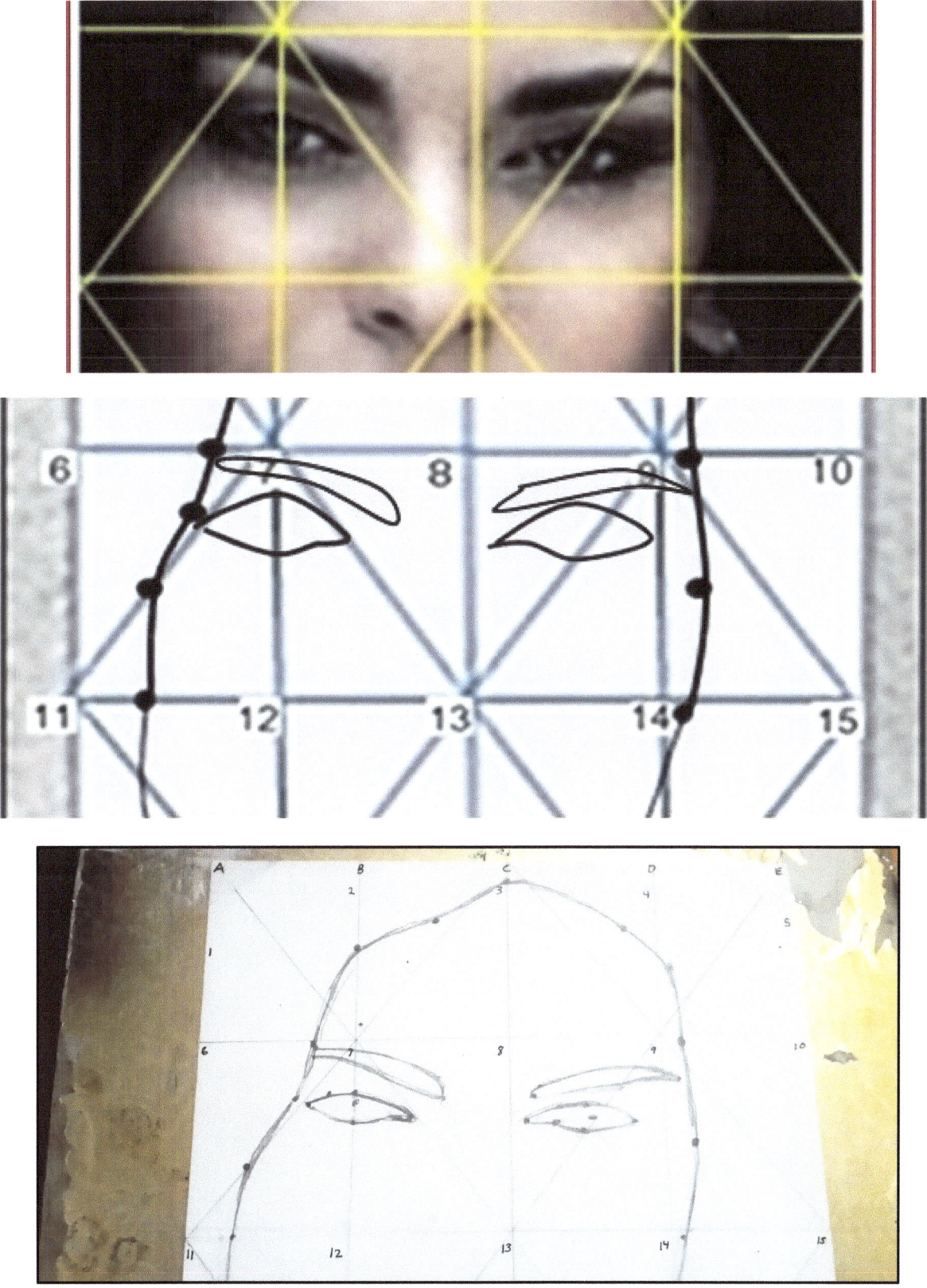

Lesson 1.0 Beginners Level

Step 13.0, next we will do the nose, but be careful because the nose shadows can confuse you. Do not add two lines to the nose or to the other side of the nose, because then the face would look more like a cartoon. Just follow along with me and you'll see you will do well.   I have also enlarged the eyes and the nose areas, so you can see better the area. Note; dot 1 and 2 will have a light line, because it's really shadows.

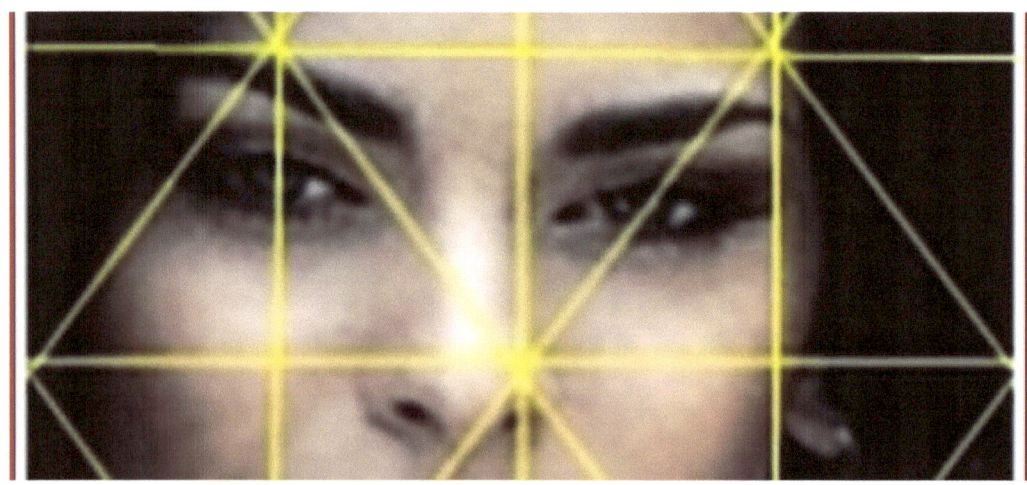

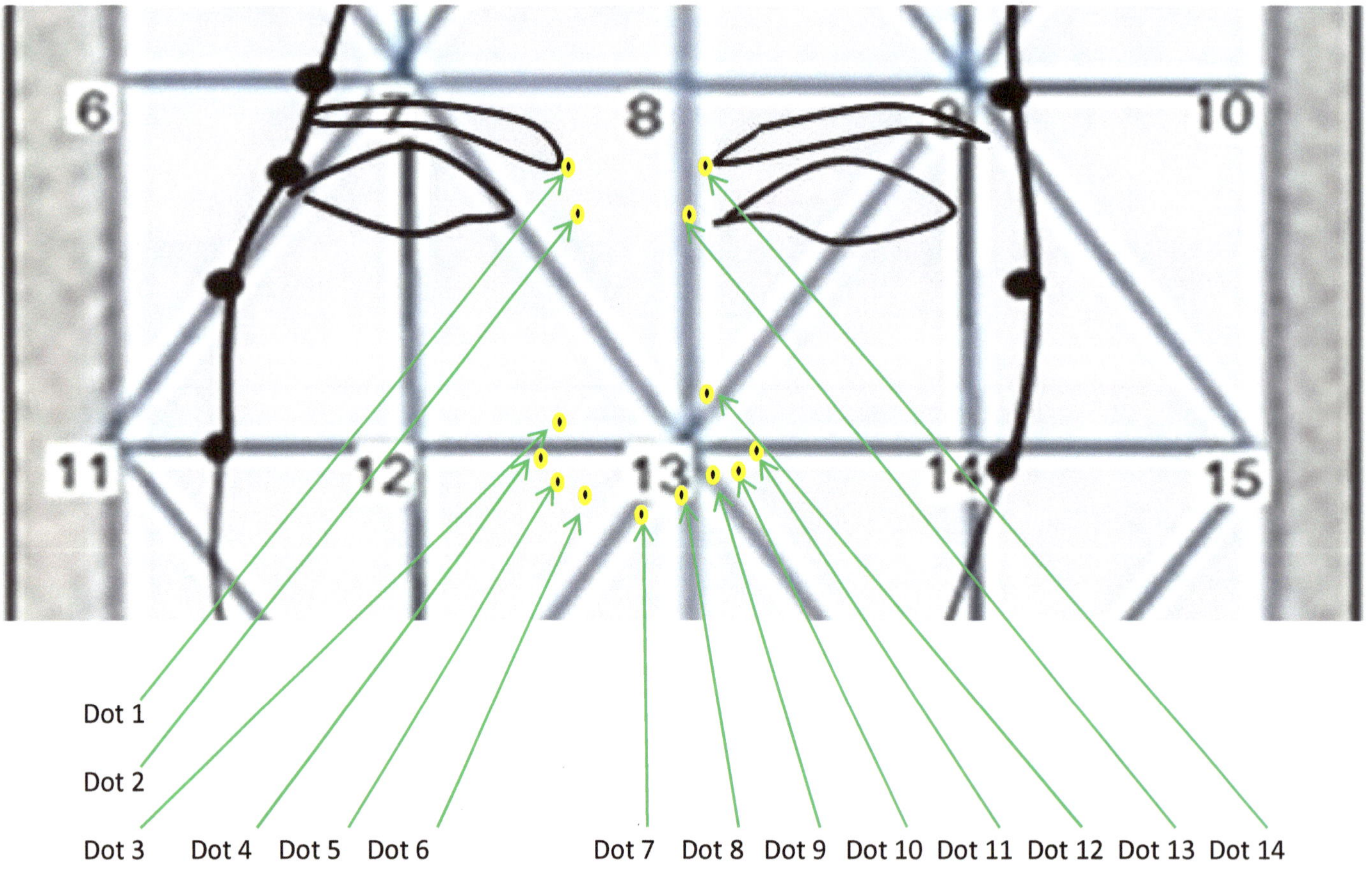

Dot 1

Dot 2

Dot 3   Dot 4   Dot 5   Dot 6   Dot 7   Dot 8   Dot 9   Dot 10   Dot 11   Dot 12   Dot 13   Dot 14

Lesson 1.0 Beginners Level

Step 14.0, now we will connect the dots, but do not connect dot 2 with dot 3 and do not connect dot 6 with dot 7. Note, you would need to add the nose opening as you see on my drawing.

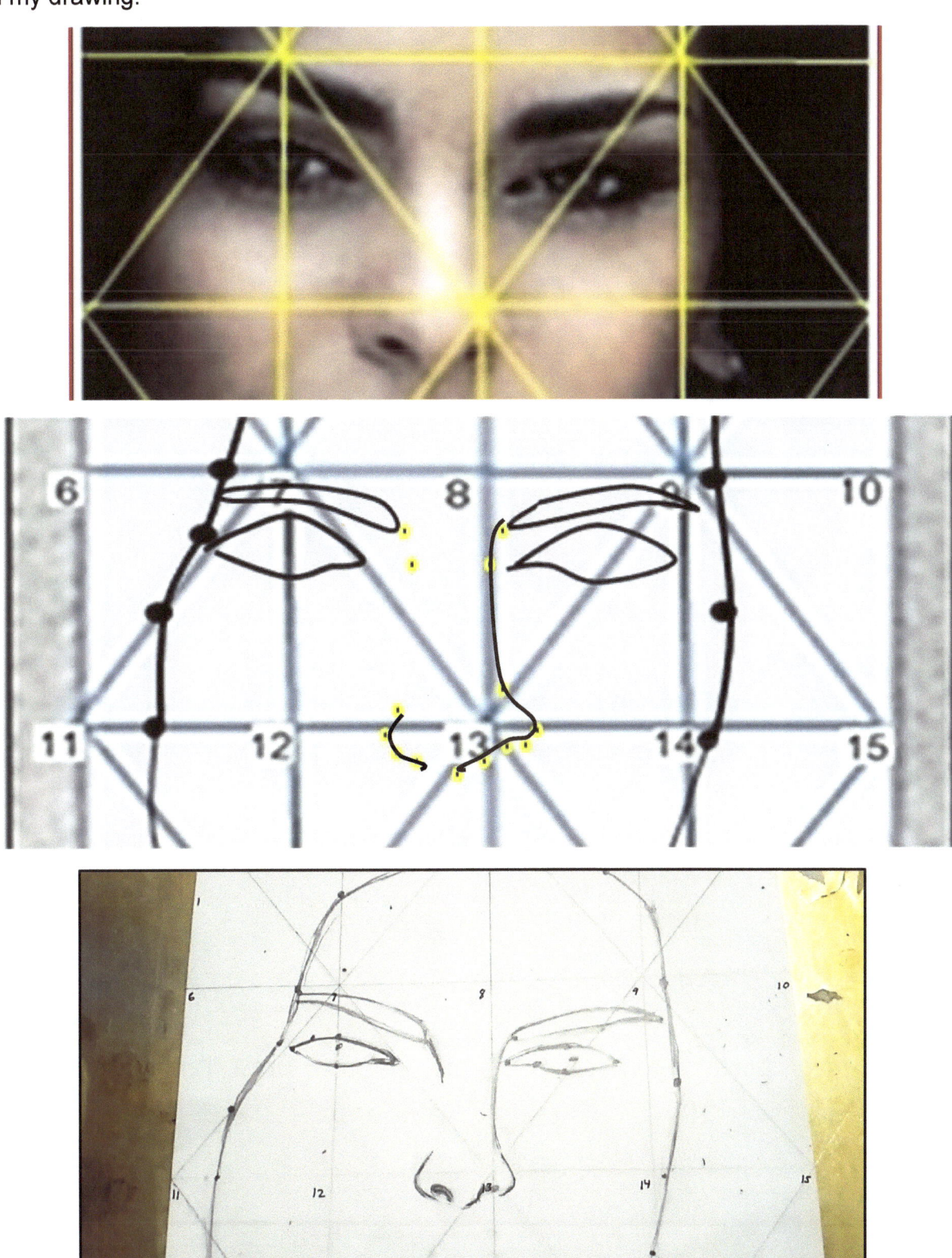

Lesson 1.0 Beginners Level

Step 15.0, next we will do the mouth.

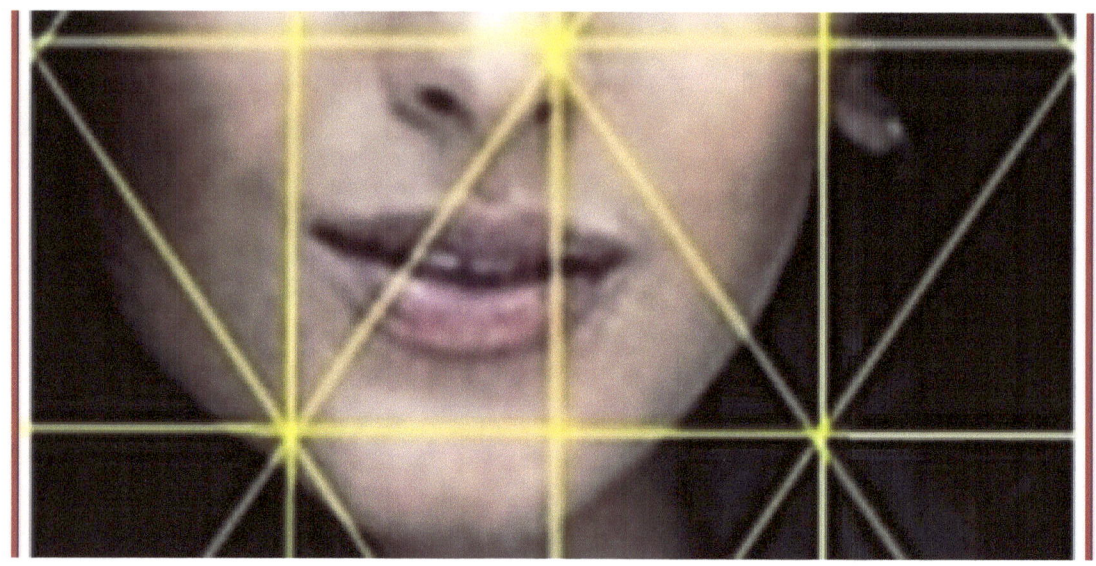

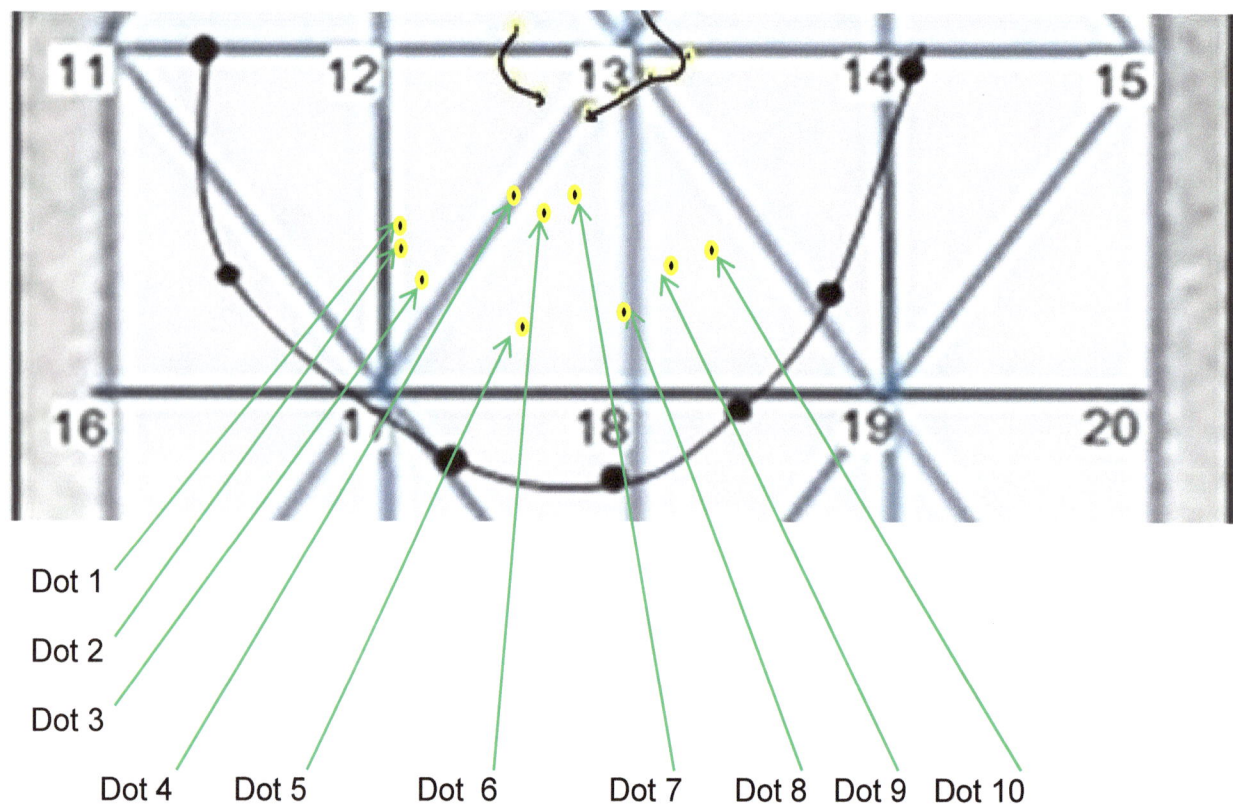

Dot 1

Dot 2

Dot 3

Dot 4   Dot 5   Dot 6   Dot 7   Dot 8   Dot 9   Dot 10

Lesson 1.0 Beginners Level

Step 16.0, before we connect the dots we put the dot go inside the month.

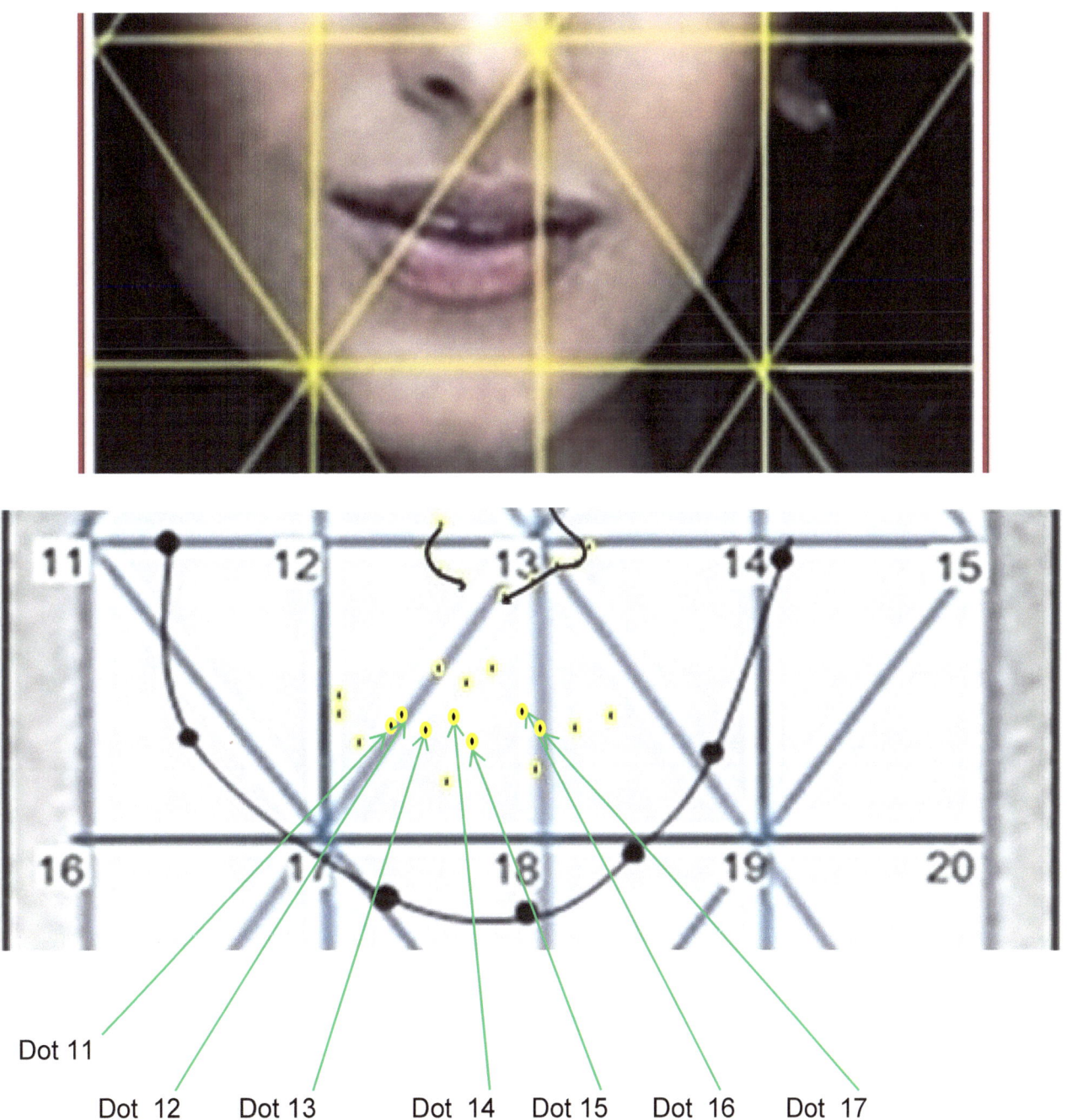

Dot 11

Dot 12   Dot 13   Dot 14   Dot 15   Dot 16   Dot 17

Lesson 1.0 Beginners Level

Step 17.0, now we will connect the dots.

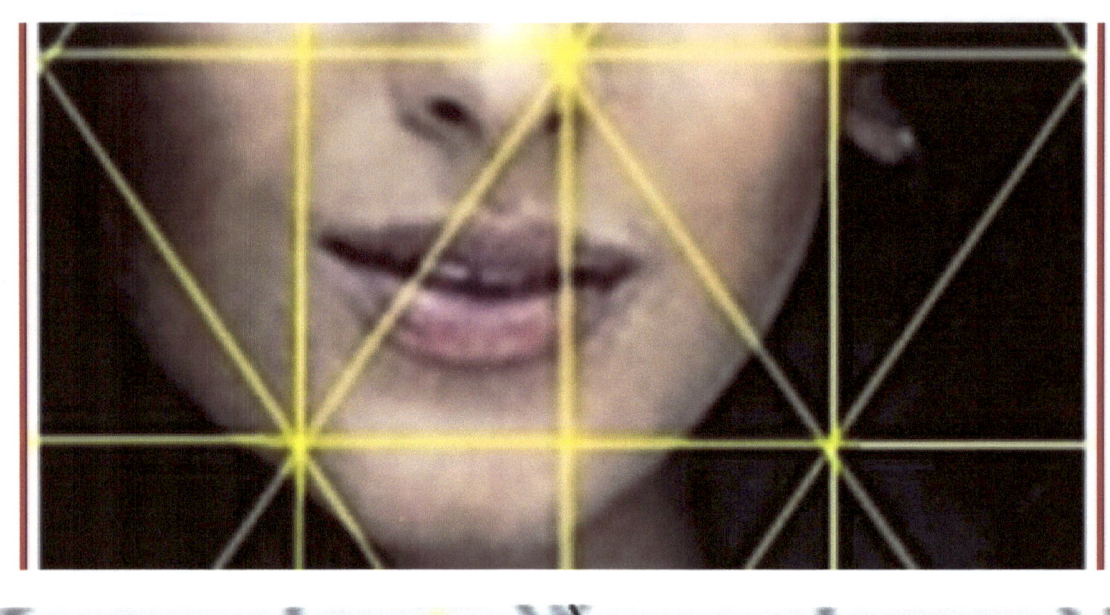

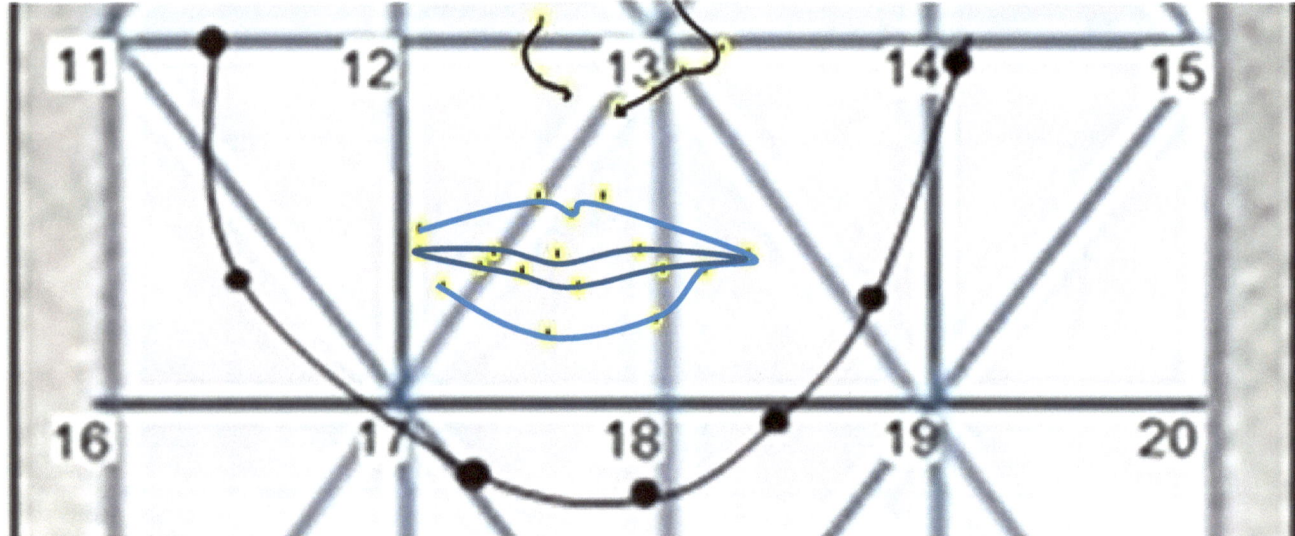

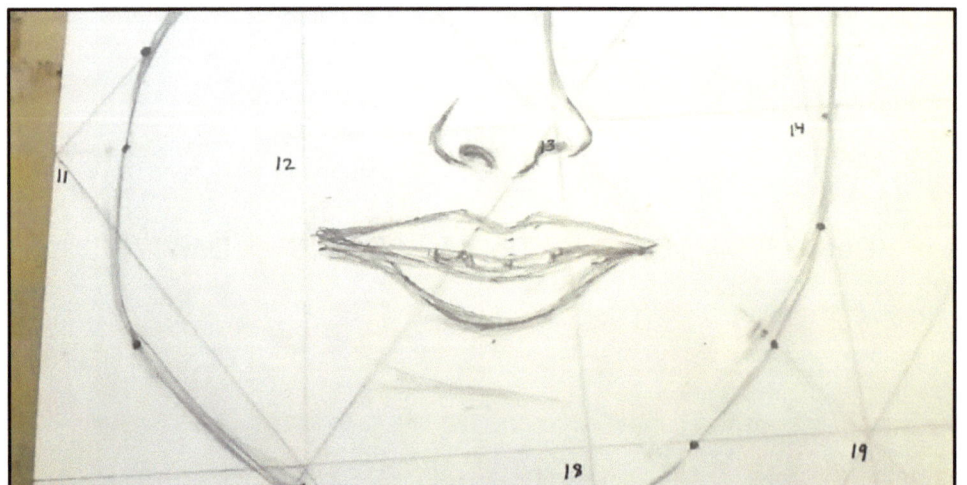

Now you can see what you should have completed, however you may be seeing that the drawing you did may not look a lot like the photo your using. So, because I don't know what your drawing or how it's coming out I would use my drawing to explain why maybe you're drawing don't seem the same as the photo you are using to do your drawing.

At this step what you should have is just the lines of your face without the shadows. Because the face doesn't have the shadows the face looks wider than the photo. Also the eyes look smaller than the photo, because the eyes are missing details, such as the eyelid and eyelashes. The pupil of the eye is done all you should have is the dot.

Before moving to Lesson 2.0 Soft Details, you should take the time to review your drawing and look for mistakes. On my drawing there is an intentional mistake on the hair line that I may, so you can see how much of a difference a small mistake can make in a face drawing. If you doing the drawing I have been doing you'll need to fix this mistake.

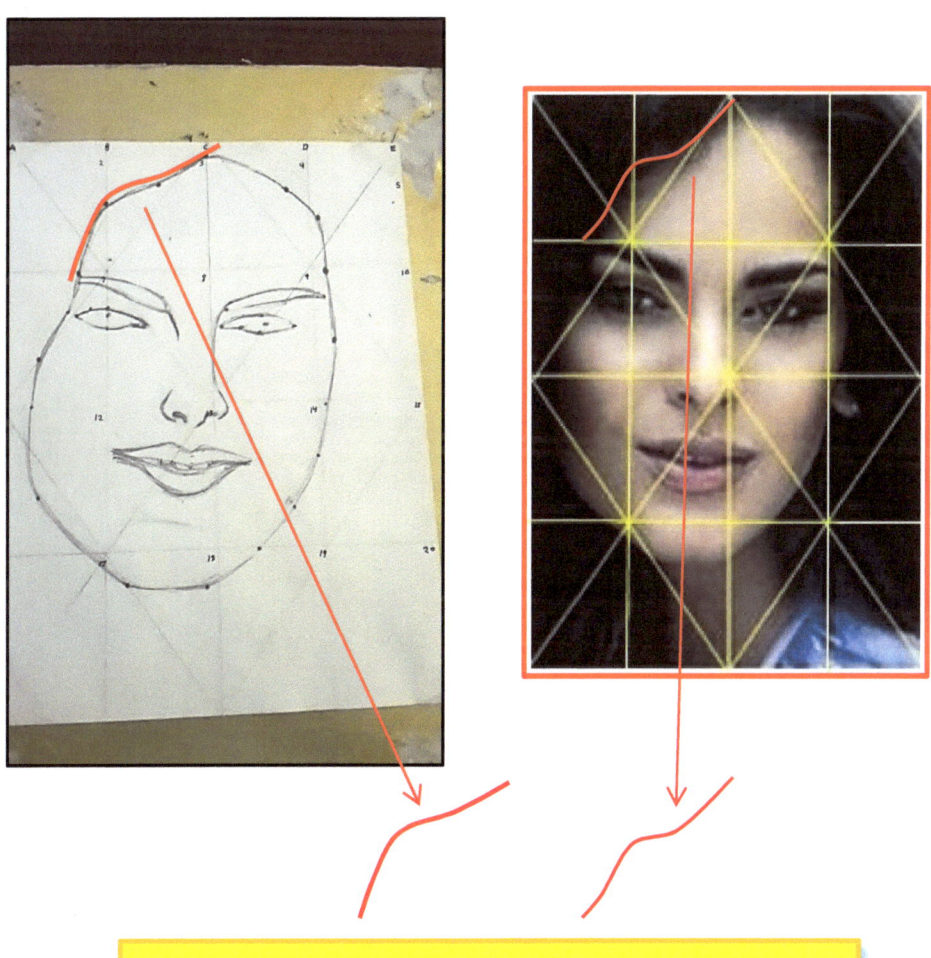

Here you'll see the two lines are not the same.

Lesson 2.0 Soft Details

Now you can see the mistake fixed and the difference it does to the drawing. On this lesson you will learn how to add the details and how to ad shadows to your drawing to give it the life it needs in order to make your drawing look great. Up to now you may have been using a number two pencil. On this lesson you still may need your number two pencil, but you should have a darker pencil or a pencil with a greater number. Having darker pencils will allow you to do the darker areas on the face. You should also have some tissue paper and some white drawing paper. Note; we will keep working on the same drawing you're doing and the white drawing paper will only be used to make the shadow mix blend.

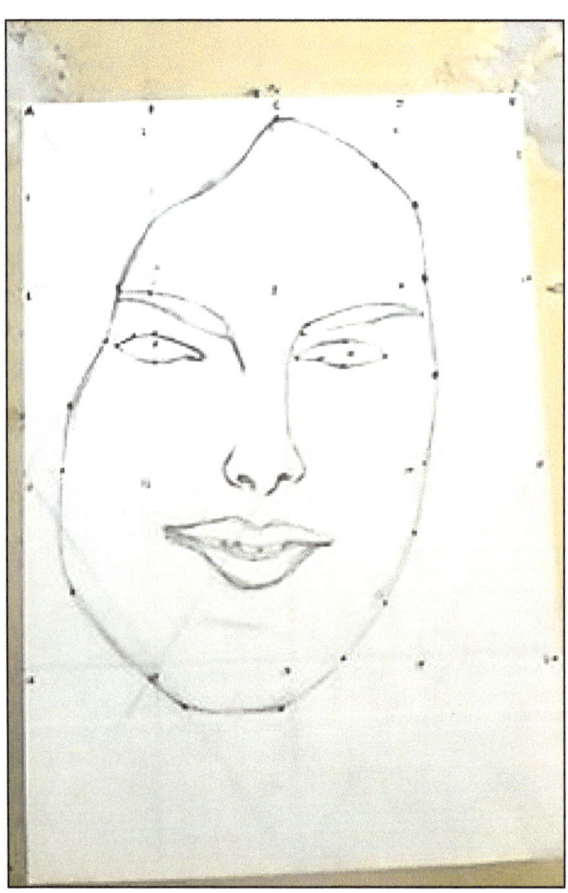
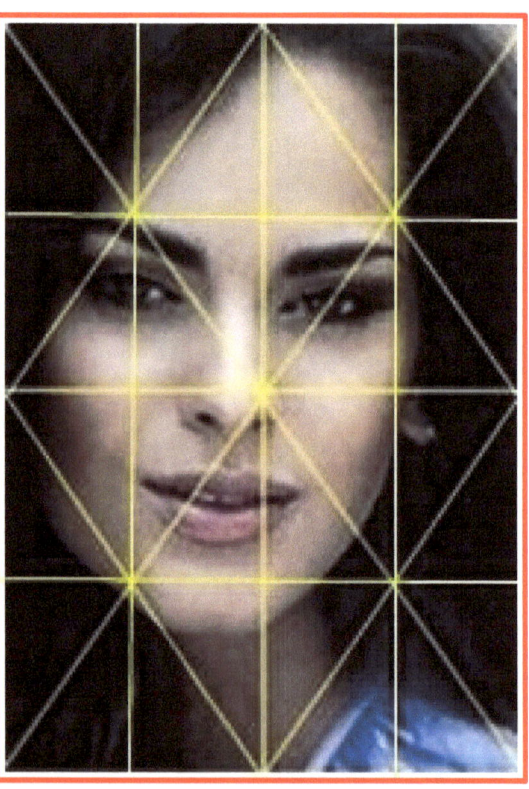

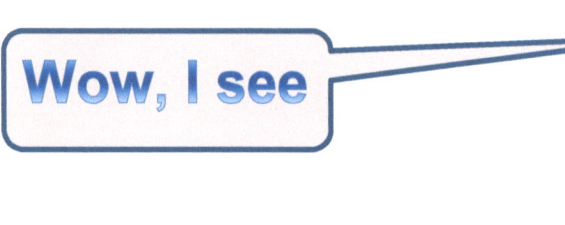

Lesson 2.0 Soft Details

The tissue paper is use under your drawing hand when you are working on your drawing. By using tissue paper it will help to prevent smears on your drawing.

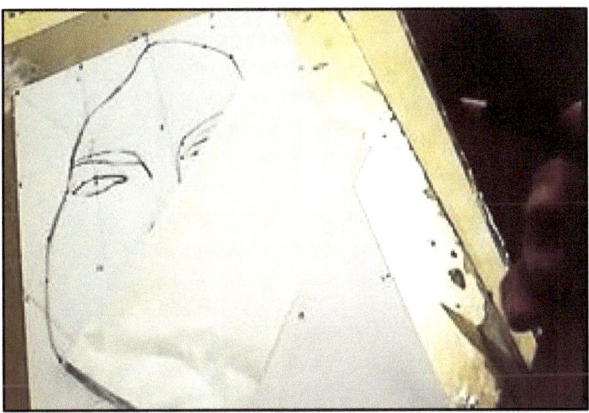 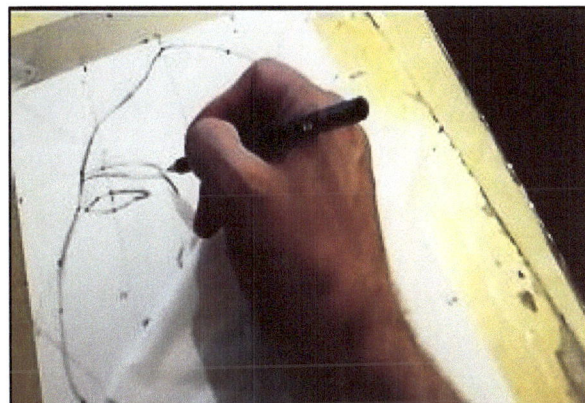

Step 1.0, you will now fill in the eyebrows with your dark pencil. When filling in the eyebrows you will need to move your pencil up or down or in the direction of the eyebrows hair flow, so you can get a realistic look to the eyebrows. Note; any lines, dots, or numbers within the area your filling in would need to be erase and if the outline of the eyebrow is too dark you should erase it, so you can barely see it before you fill in the eyebrow.

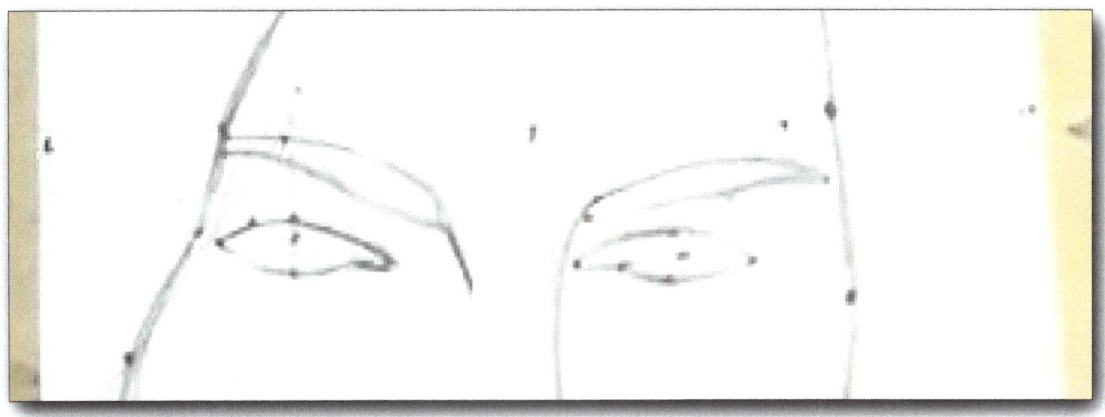

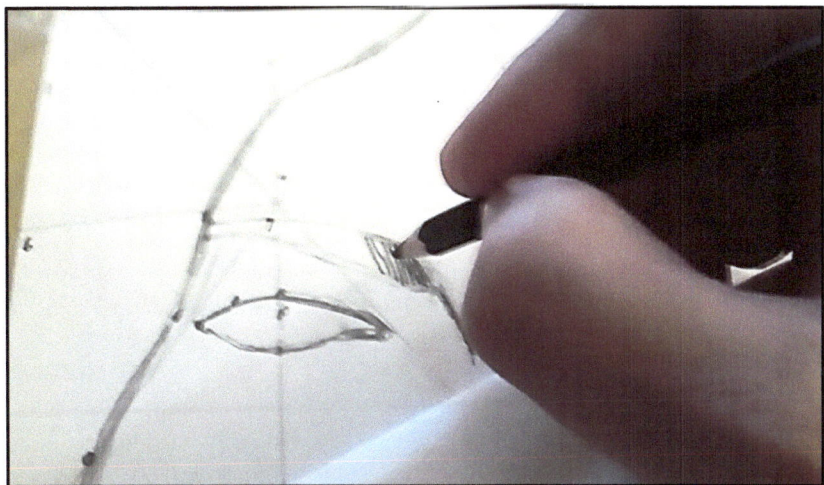

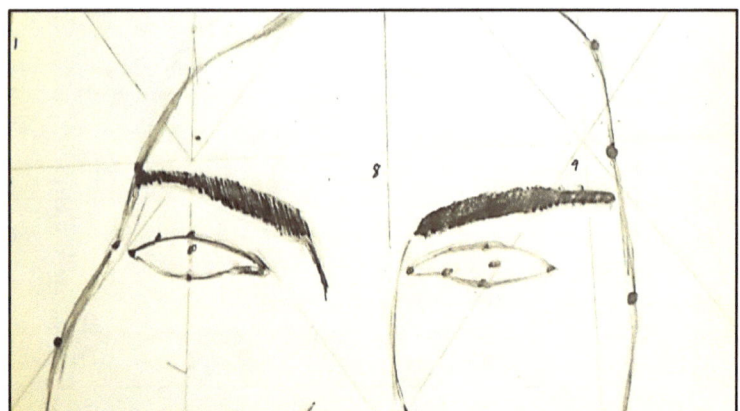

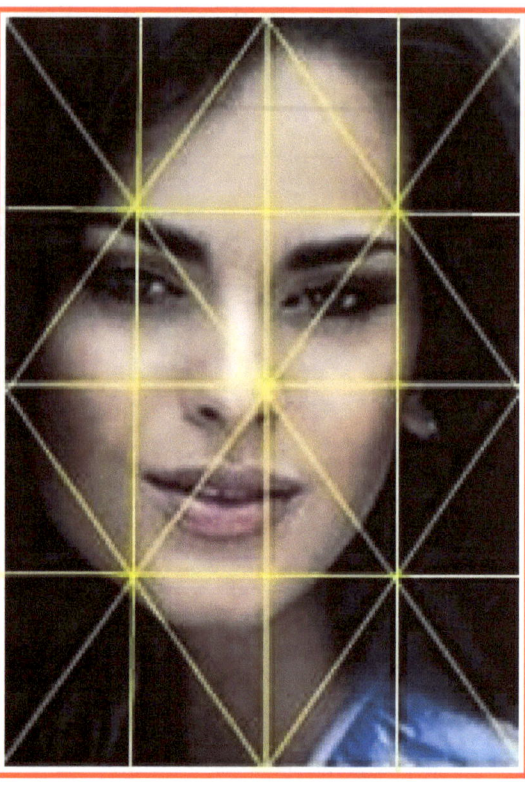

Lesson 2.0 Soft Details

Step 2.0, next fill in within the mouth areas, but be careful with the teeth and lips. Use your dark pencil and don't forget to use the tissue paper under your drawing hand. Also, erase any line within the areas you're going to fill and if the lip lines are too dark you'll need to make then lighter by erasing them lightly.

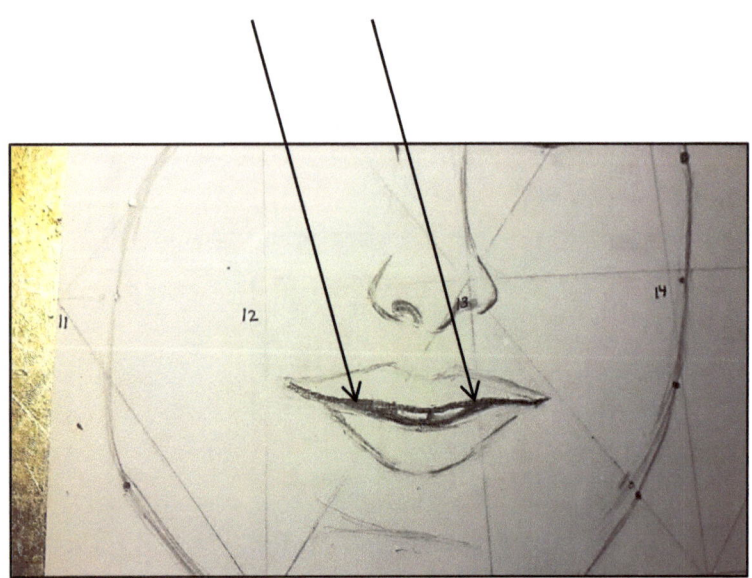

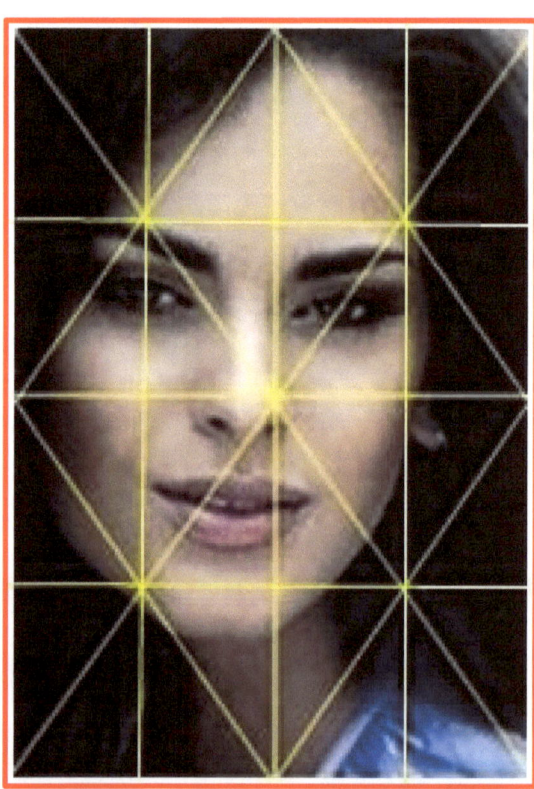

Lesson 2.0 Soft Details

Step 3.0, next we will work on the eyes and it's very important to understand that the eye can make or break your drawing. You will be using the number two pencil for this step. Making one eye bigger than the other would look very bad, or not having the eye in the right place would make your eyes look cross-eyeded.

Make sure to erase any line or dots within the areas you're going to be working on each eye and make the light lines lighter on the lip if their too dark. Also, if the eye lines are too dark you'll need to make then lighter by erasing them lightly.

Note; you should have a dot in the eye pupil already, but make sure it's in the right place by looking at the model's photo and lines on your drawing paper and the photo.

Frist you should make the eye pupils and then make the eyeballs around the eye pupils.

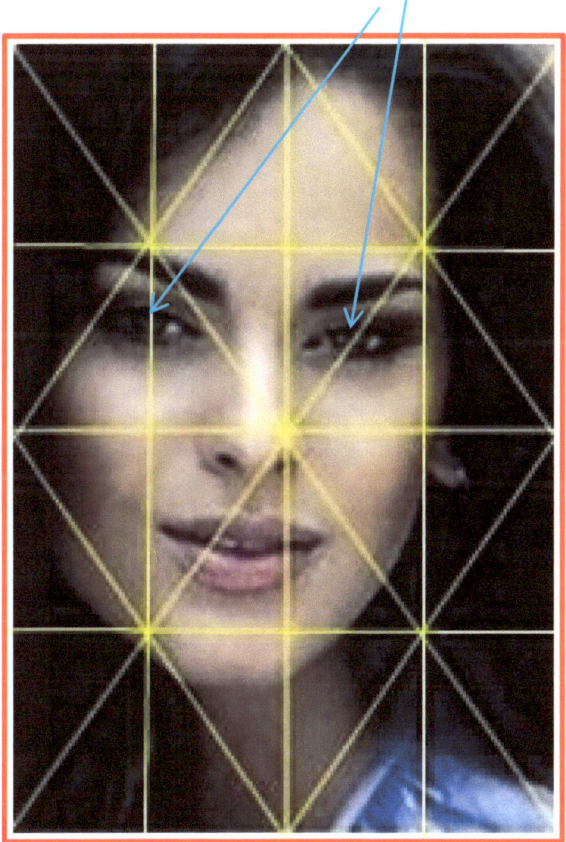

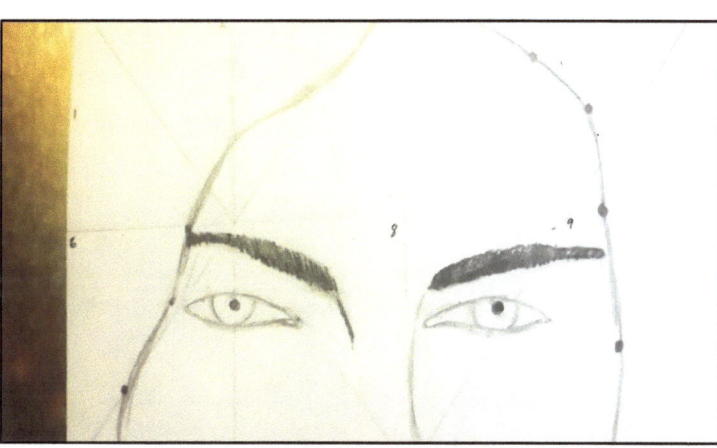

Lesson 3.0 Details and Shadows.

In this lesson we will do the detailing and shadowing to bring your drawing to life. Some of you may fine this stage to be a bit intimidating, but I can assure you the lines will help you and it shouldn't be a problem. Here is a shadow scale I develop that we will use to do this drawing and once you learn this scale you can use it to help you in your other drawings. The scale range is from 1-500, 1 being white and 500 being black.

Step 1.0, we will use super lite dots to make the areas of the shadows and the number two pencil. Note; this will seem like a lot of dots, but this is my way to teach you, but once you have an understanding how the lines help you, you will not need to make the dots and only lines. And when you're very good you'll make the shadows without having to make dots or lines.

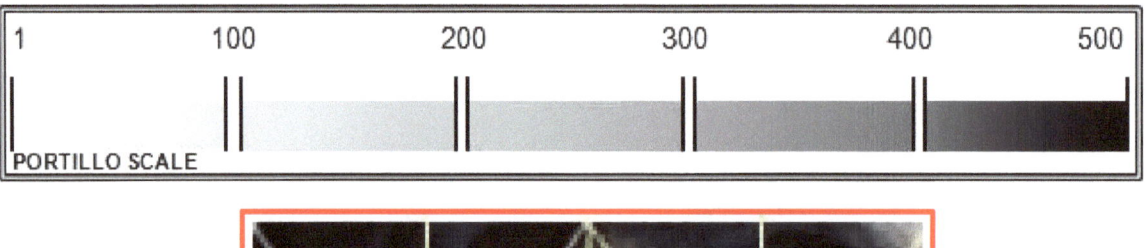

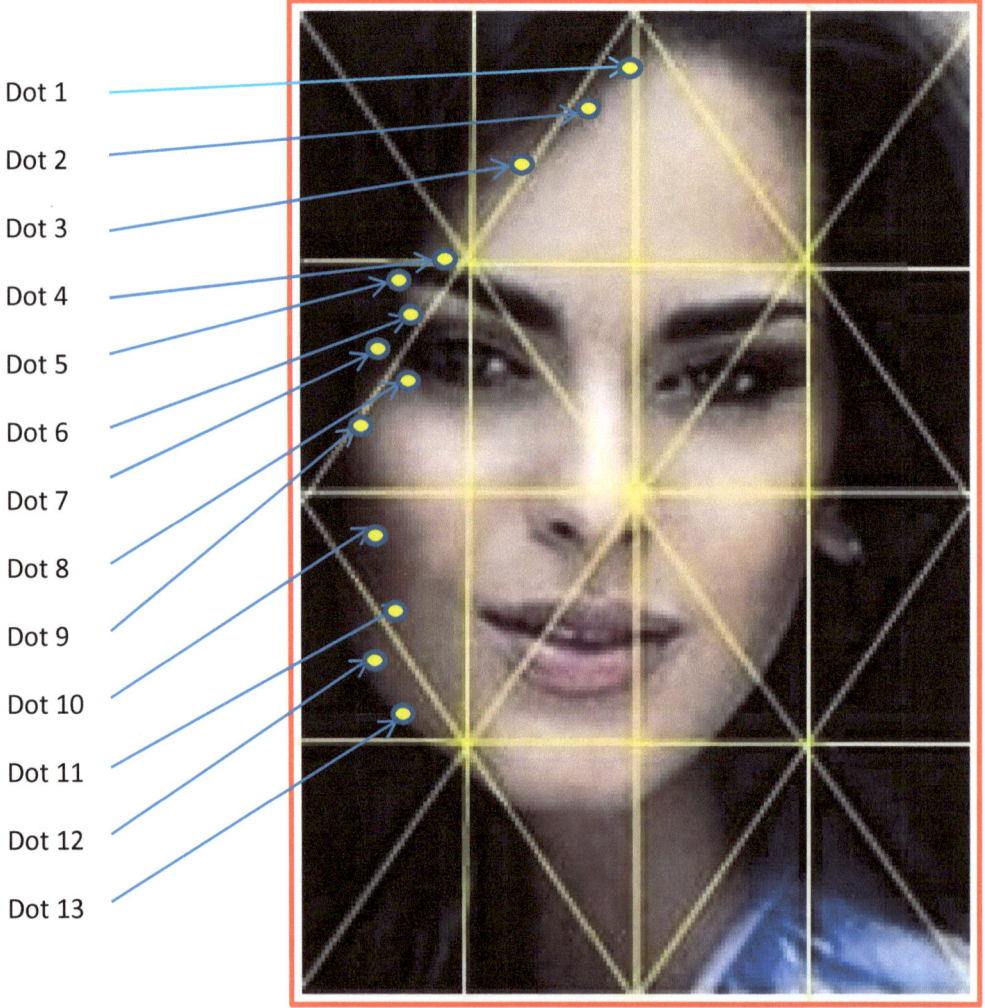

Lesson 3.0 Details and Shadows.

Here I have place the photo with the lines and the one without the lines, so I can show you what we're looking for. Note; the light is coming from somewhere on top left of the face, so the shadows are on the right of the face. But, you will all see some shadows on the left of her face, because of her hire casting a shadow. This is only the first layer of shadows of the right side of her face.

Here I have lineout the shadows.

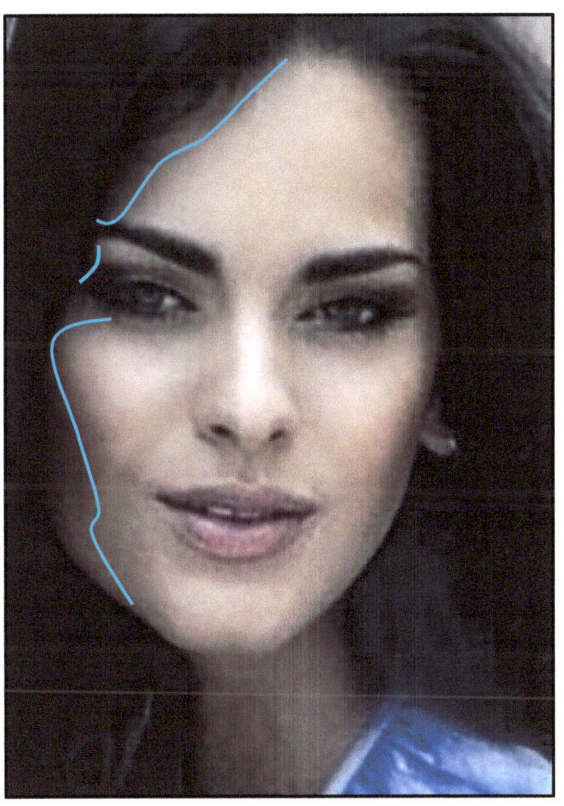
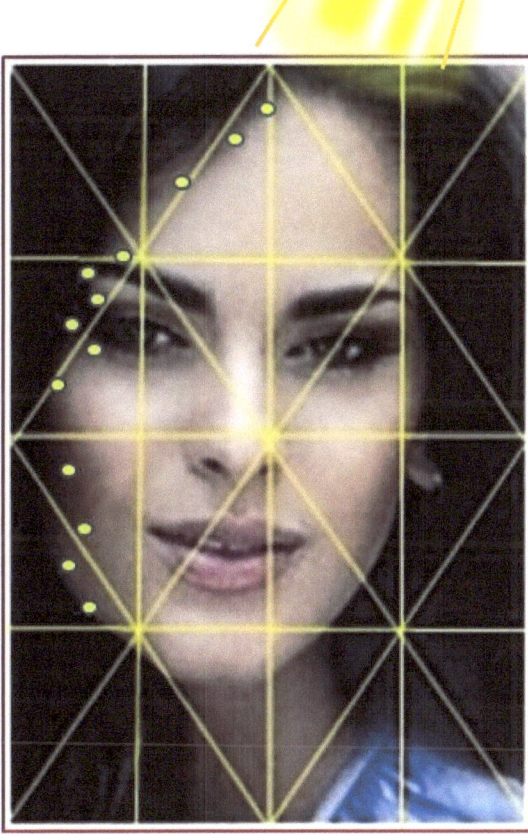

Lesson 3.0 Details and Shadows.

Step 2.0, we will now use the scale to get an idea how light or dark is the shadow in the areas.

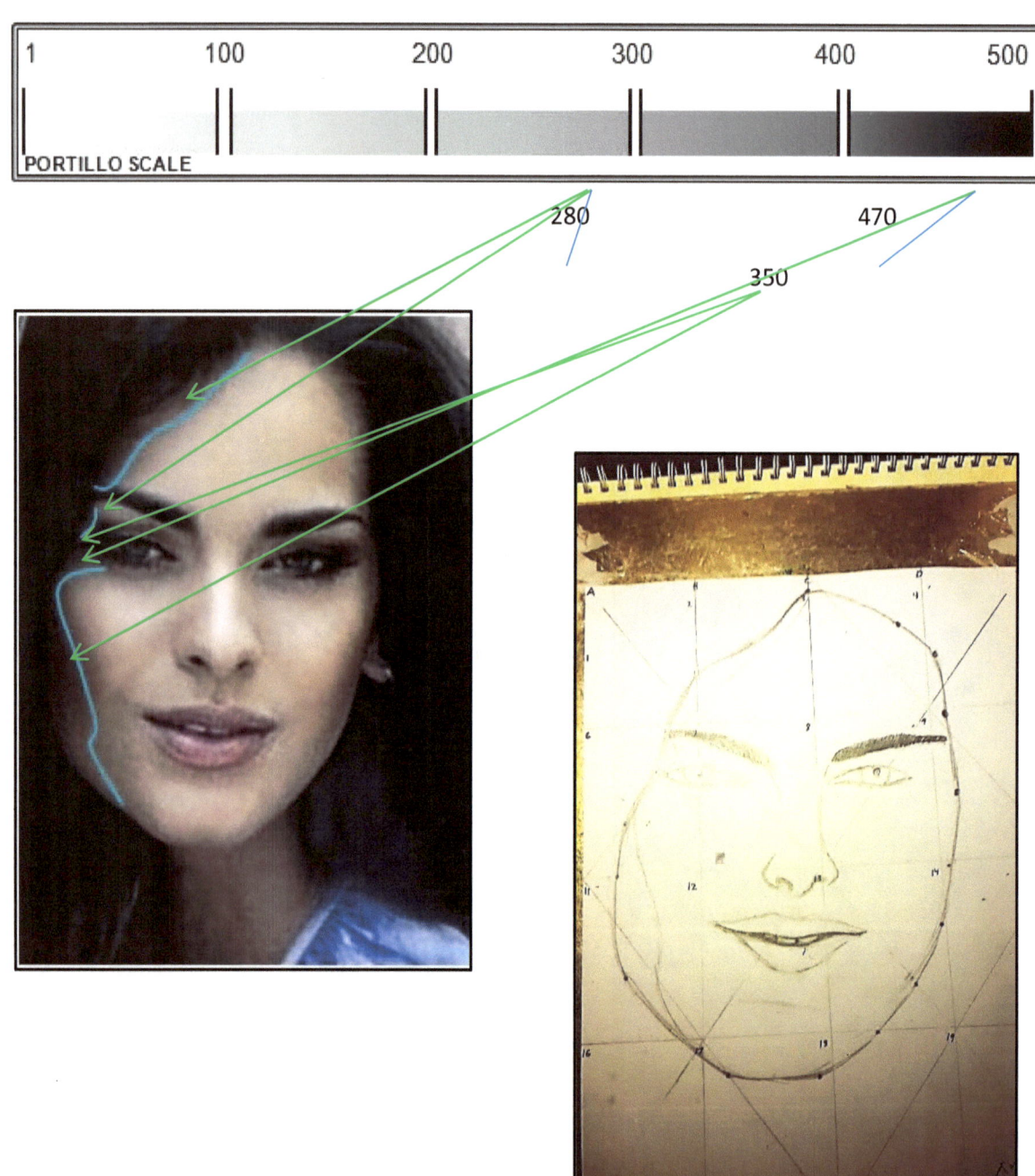

Lesson 3.0 Details and Shadows.

Step 2.1, before we can start on this step you will need to get a paper so we mix the shadow blend using your number two pencil and your dark pencil.

Frist take your dark pencil and fill in an area about 1 ½ inches wide dragging your pencil led back and forth as you see below.

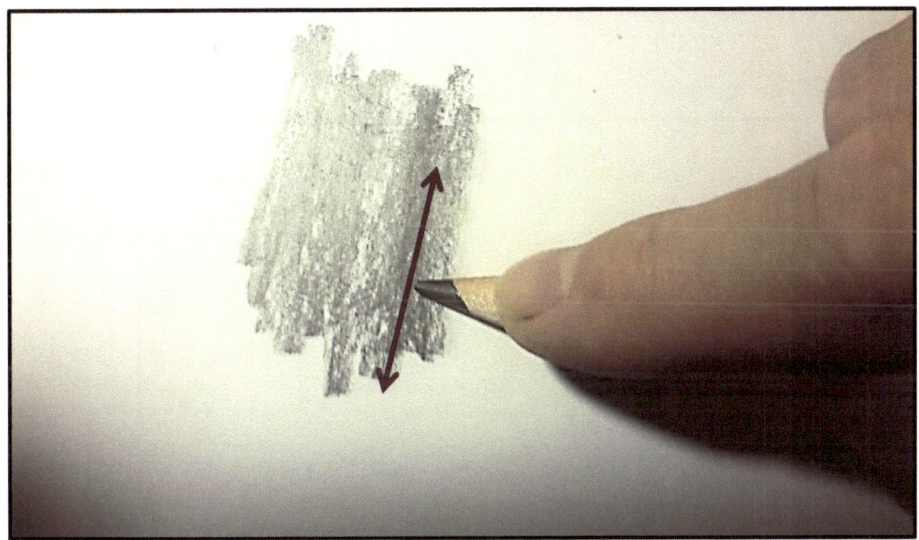

Then next to the area you fill in with your dark pencil you'll then use your number two pencil and do the same thing, but you'll need to overlap the dark pencil area a little.

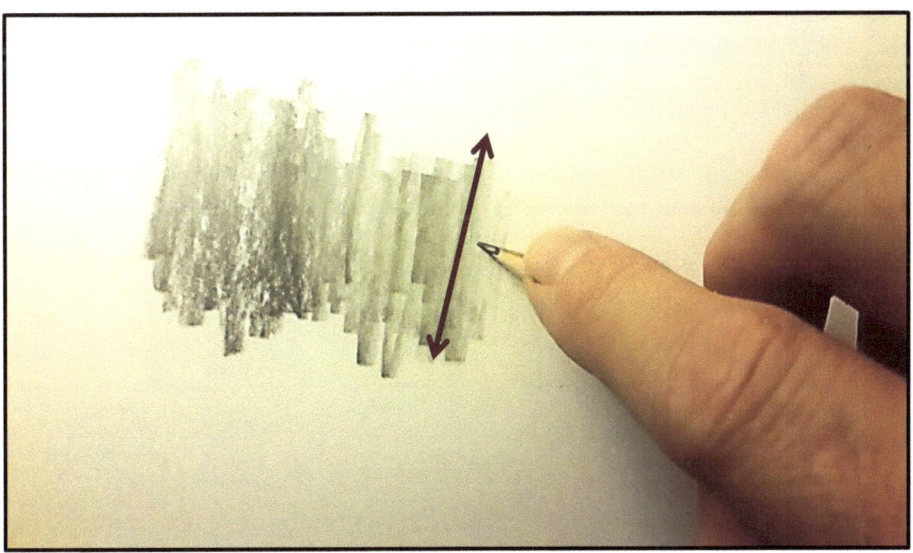

Lesson 3.0 Details and Shadows.

Step 2.2, we will use our fingers to applied and fill in the shadow areas on the face. This technique of using your fingers to fill in and applied the colors is very old school and easy to do.

Note; there is no lead in your pencil your pencil only contains graphite. So just wash your hands when you're done.

At about the middle of the mix slide your finger back and forth on the mix until you have some on your finger.

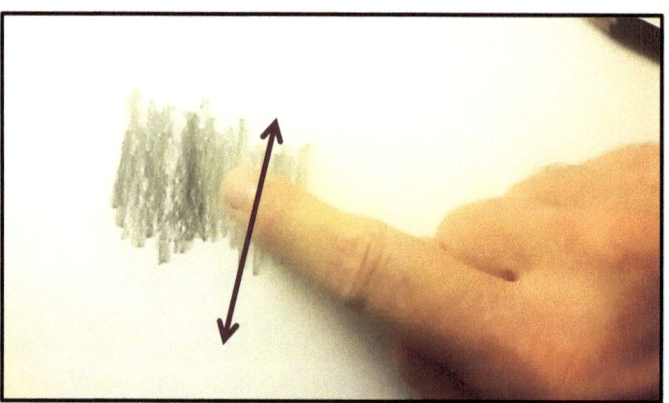

Step 2.3, Make sure to erase any line or dots within the areas you're going to work on. After rubbing some graphite on your finger applied to the area and make sure you look at the scale in order to gauge the darkness of the shadow. Also you would need to start lite and apply darker as needed. When you start rubbing the graphite on to the face, start from the outer face line and work on to the inner line.

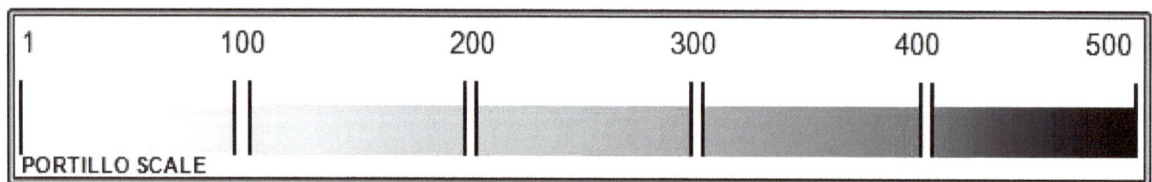

Warning; if you rub too hard or to fast you may go through the paper, or you'll ripped the paper and therefore ruining your drawing. You should start slow and work up to a safe speed.

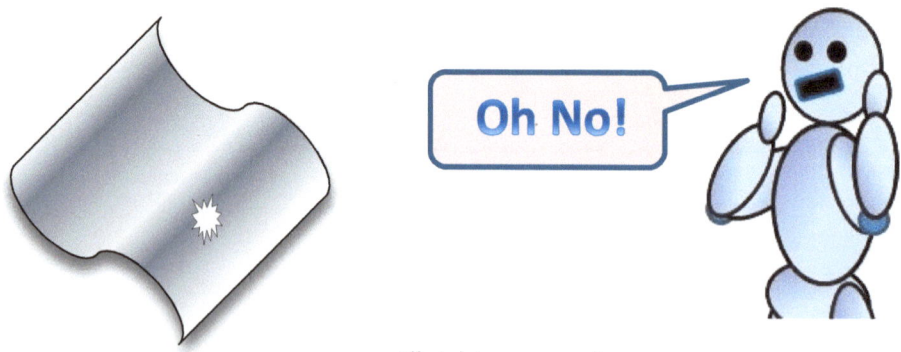

Lesson 3.0 Details and Shadows.

Step 3.0, as you get closer to the shadow line that you made you would need to erase that line, because you don't want to put your shadow color over it. The edge of the face on this photo is darker and as you get closer to the inner shadow line that you made your shadow would start getting lighter, so you are working from dark to light.

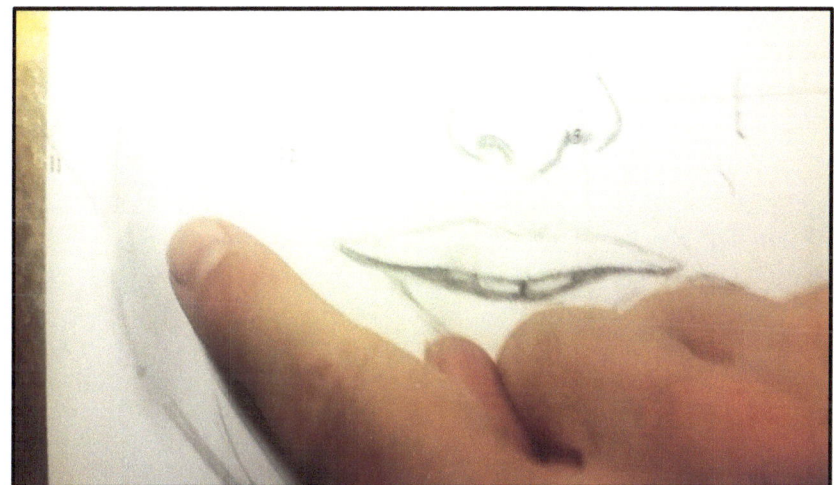

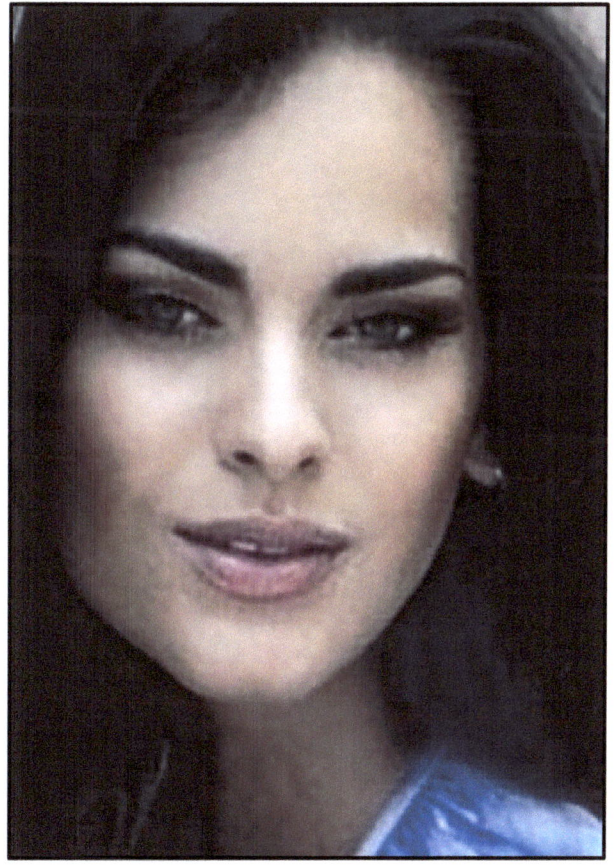

Lesson 3.0 Details and Shadows.

Step 4.0, on the right side bottom jaw it is too wide look at her photo and see my drawing 1 and you'll see the mistake on the drawing below and you'll see I fixed it.

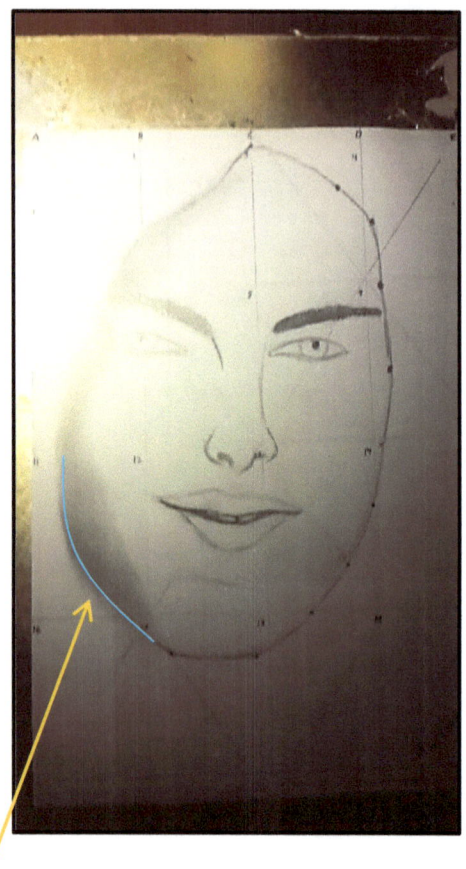

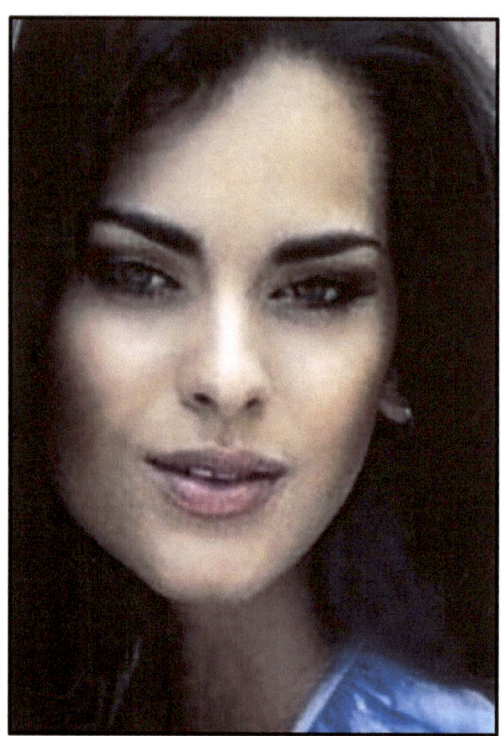

Use your eraser to cut back the area that is too wide.

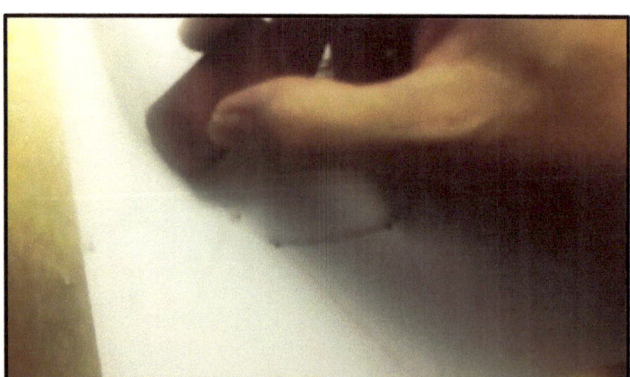

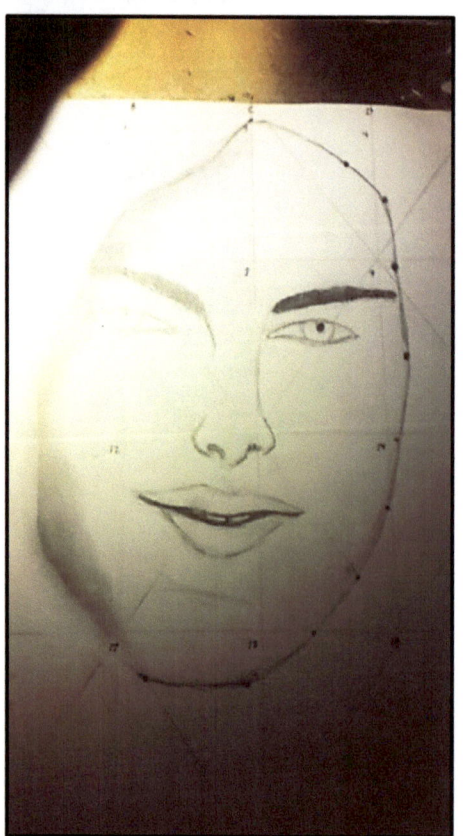

Lesson 3.0 Details and Shadows.

Step 4.1, the second layer of shadow will go on the right side of the face. We will start adding the dots and please remember to keep these dots super light. The 170 would be added to all areas within these areas. Look at the next step before you start adding the shadows, so you can understand where the shadows go.

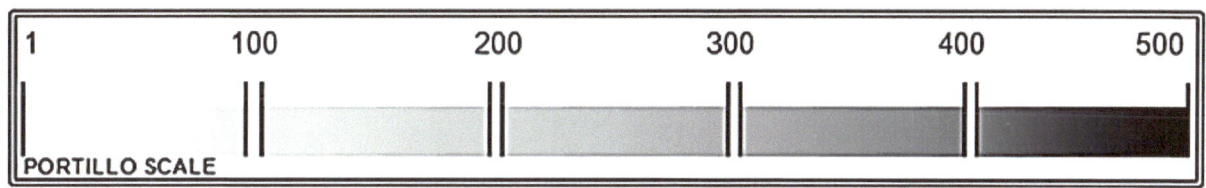

170

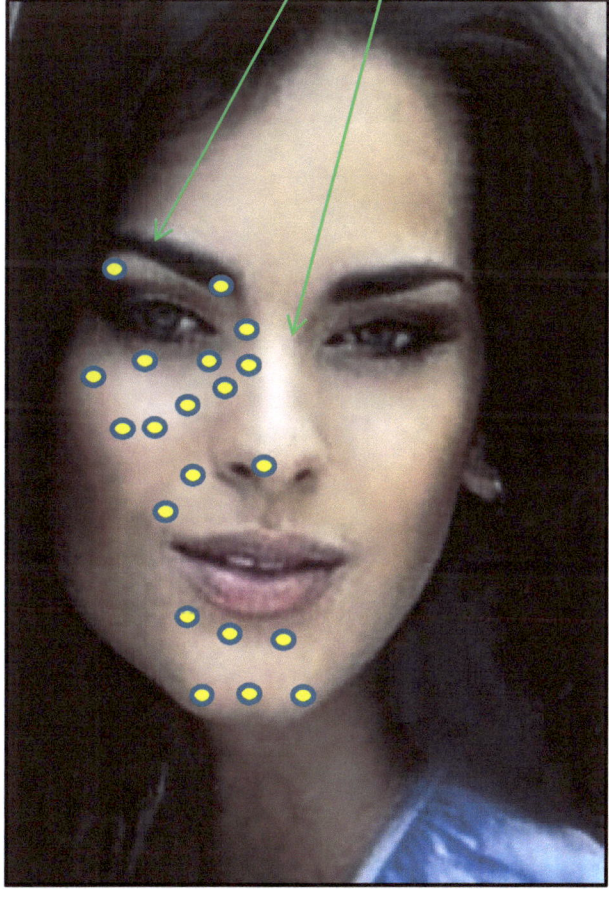
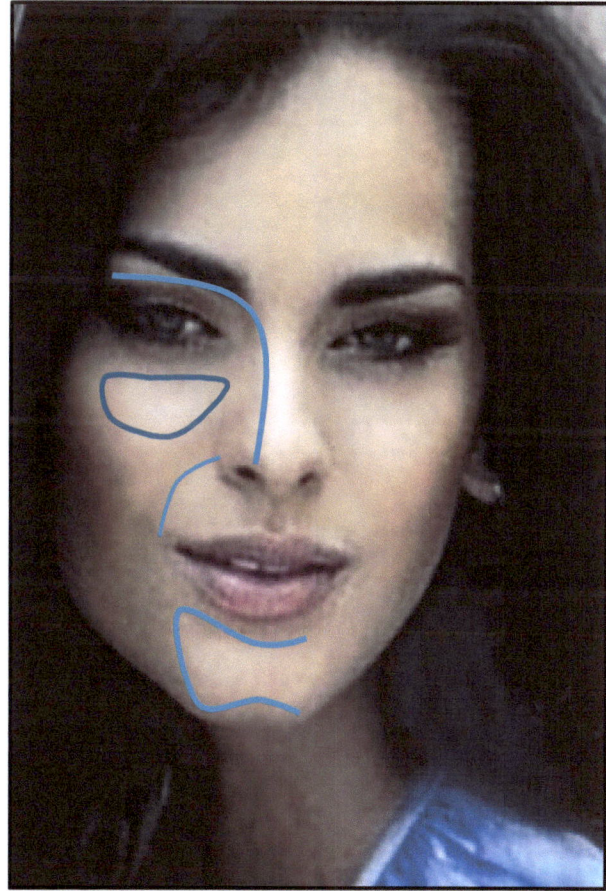

Lesson 3.0 Details and Shadows.

Step 4.2, remember before you start adding in your shadows erase the dots, lines, and numbers if you have them in the area. You should only see them barely. Note; when shadowing over the eye use your small finger and try not to get shadow within the white of the eye.

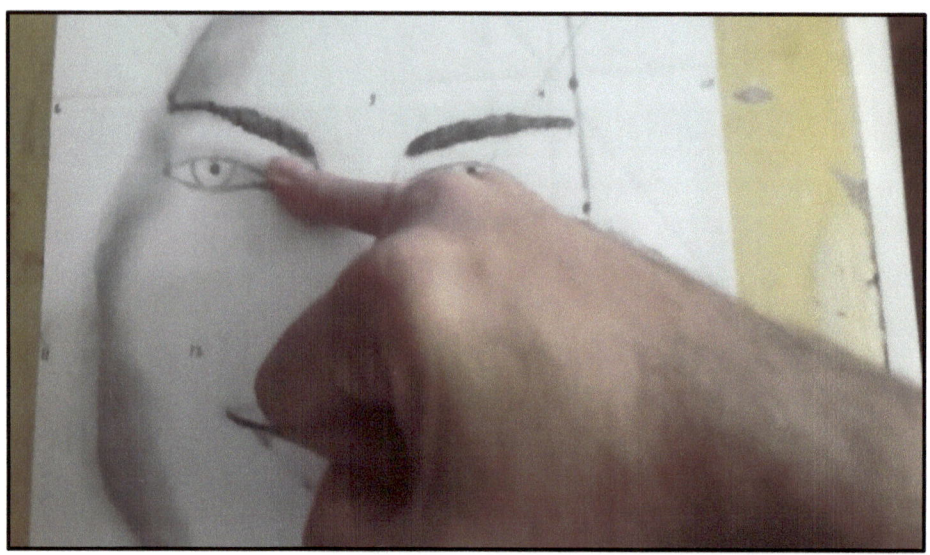

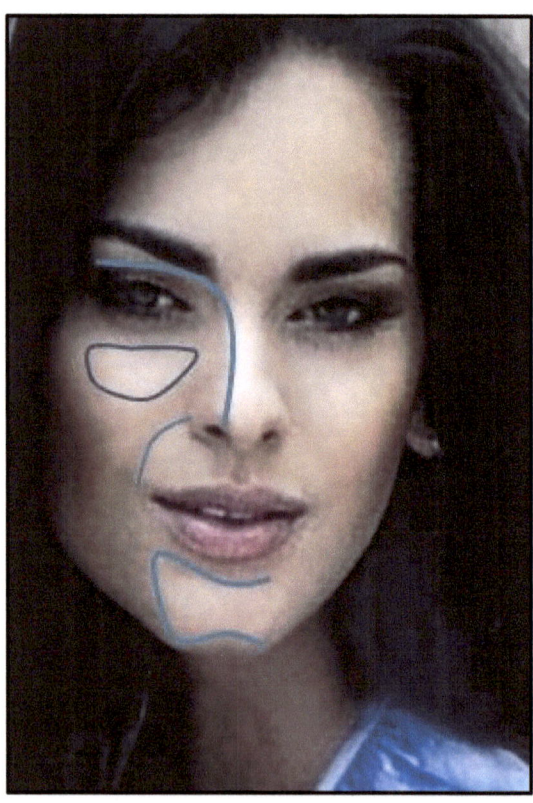

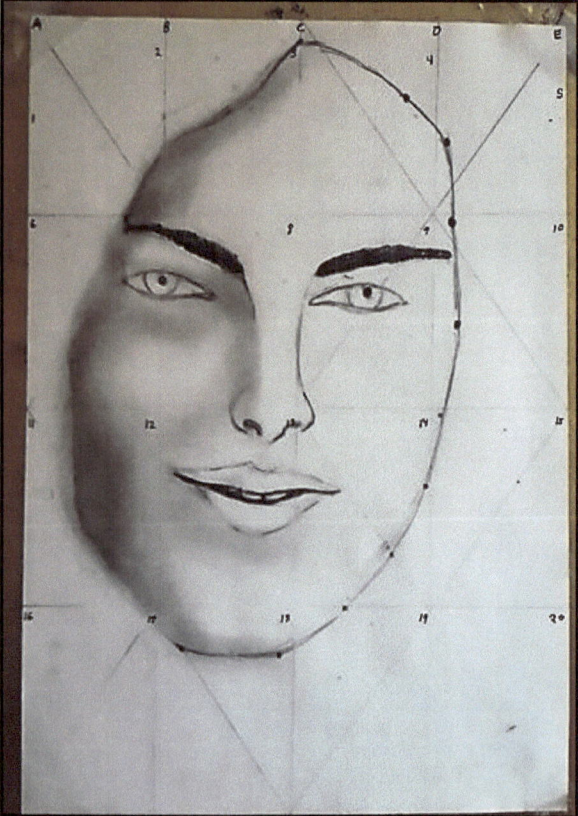

Lesson 3.0 Details and Shadows.

Step 5.0, now you will start on the other side of the face. Here I have only put the dots, now on your own you need to figure out what shade level of shadow you will be putting. You will do this on your own so you can start learning. Look at the scale to figure out what shade you need.

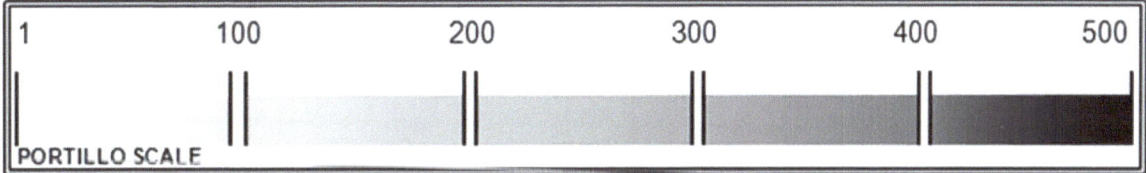

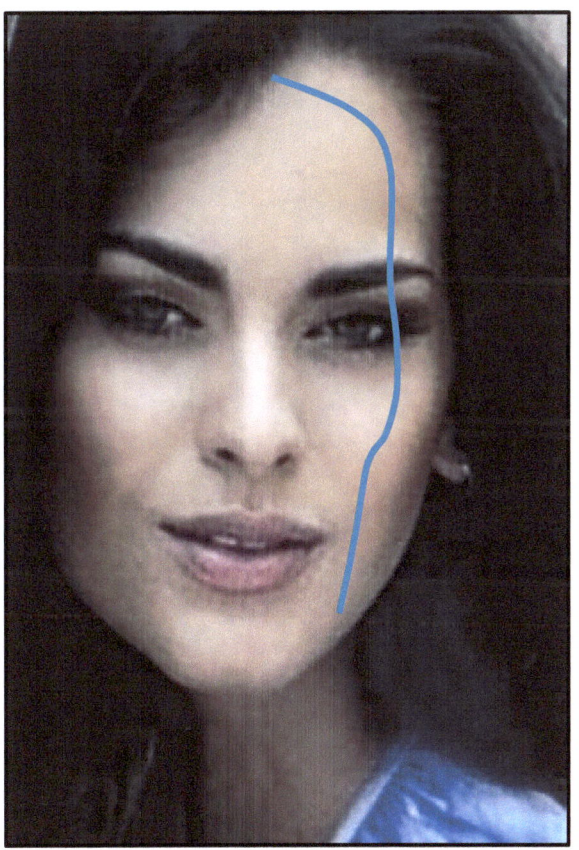 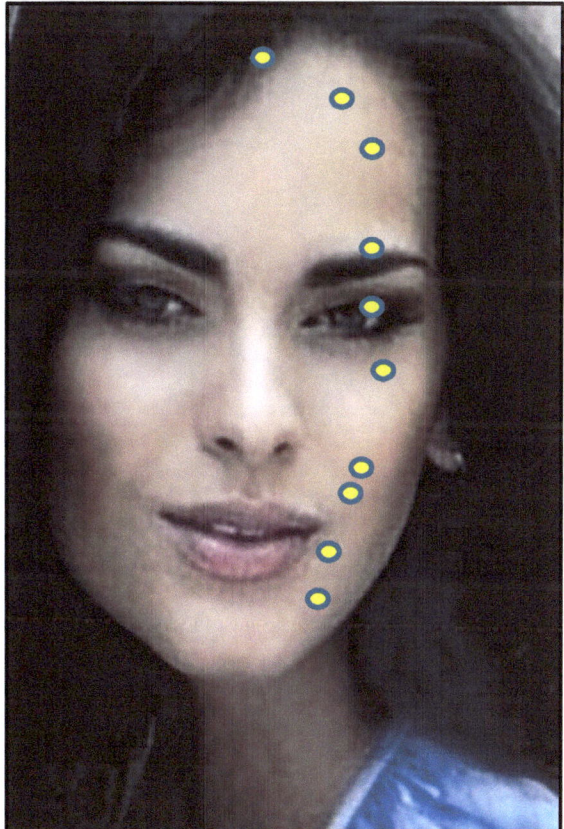

Lesson 3.0 Details and Shadows.

Step 6.0, as always remember to remove the lines, dots, and/or number from the area you're shading in. Also if the outside line of the face is too dark you will need to make it lighter. Remember you may need to make more pencil mix. Note; on my drawing for the teaching purpose of this book I have left the numbers.

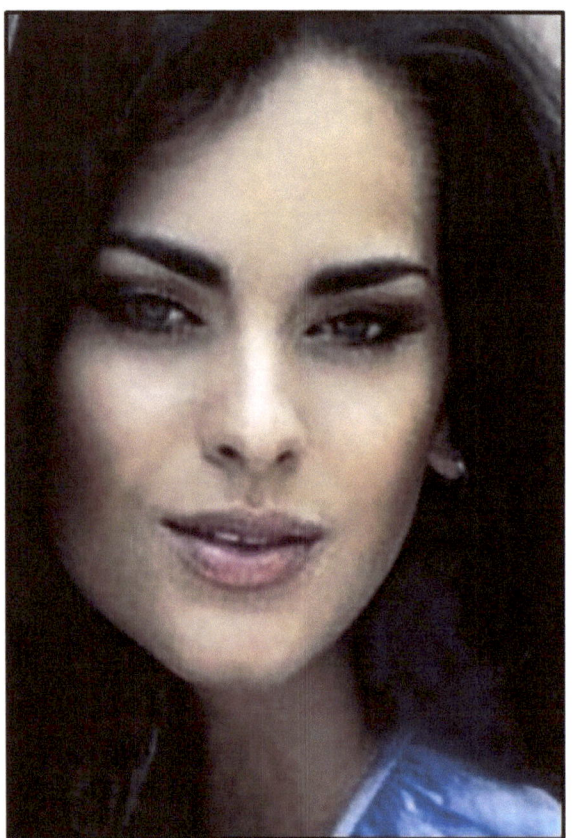
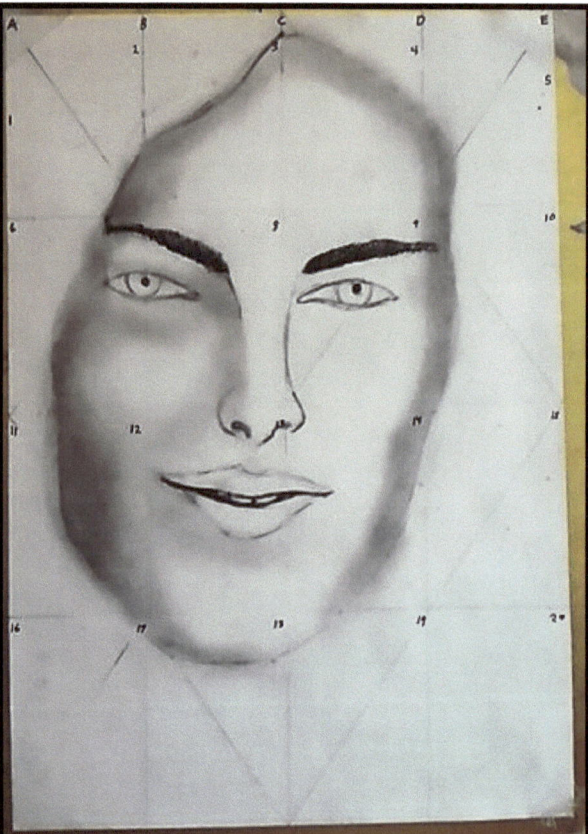

Lesson 3.0 Details and Shadows.

Step 7.0, we will now add the second layer of the shadows to the left side of the face. And as always removed all lines, numbers, and make the dot barely visible. Also, here I have only put the dots, so you would need to figure out what level of shades you will be putting. Look at the scale to help you out as needed.

Note: if the line on the left side of the nose is too dark you would need to lighten the line by lightly erasing it.

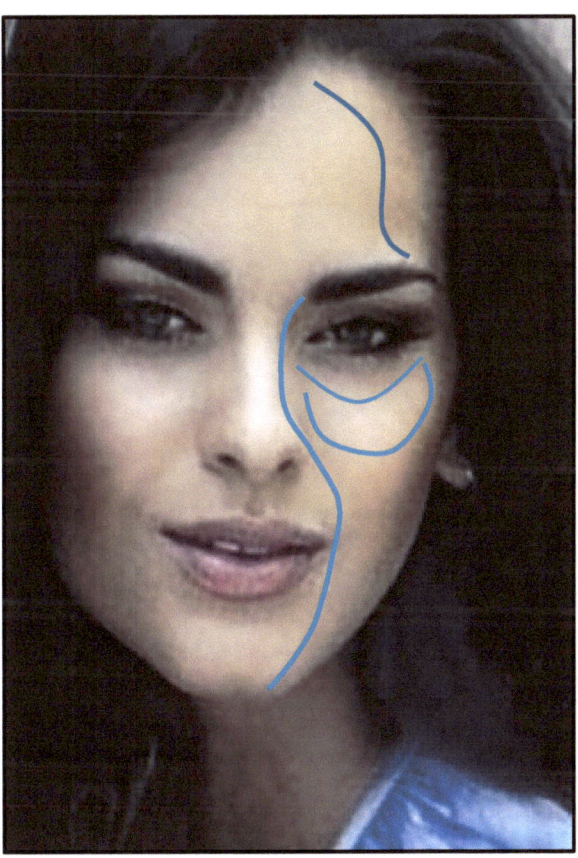 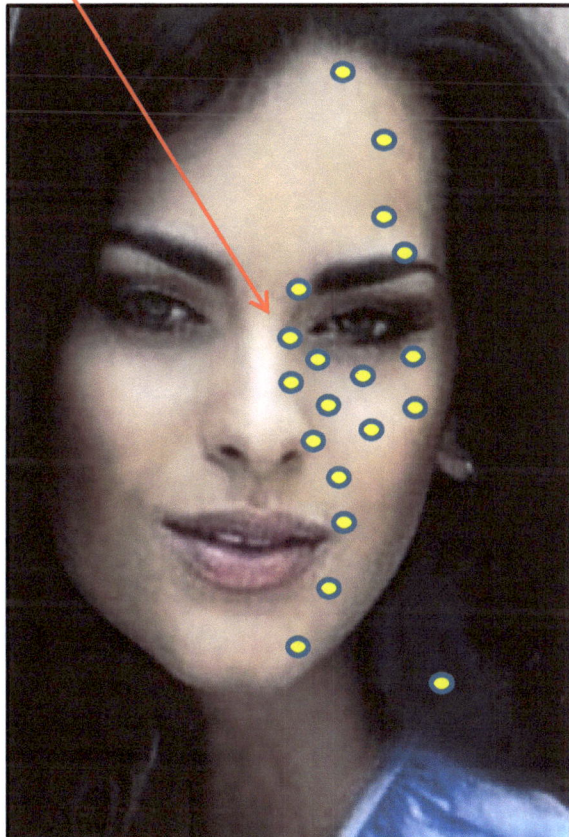

Lesson 3.0 Details and Shadows.

Step 8.0 now that you have added the second layer you need to review your shadows levels and check for areas that are too light or too dark and make the adjustments.

In the nose areas on my drawing there are some areas that need fixing. One is the line on the upper nose that is too dark and the other area is at the tip of the noes.

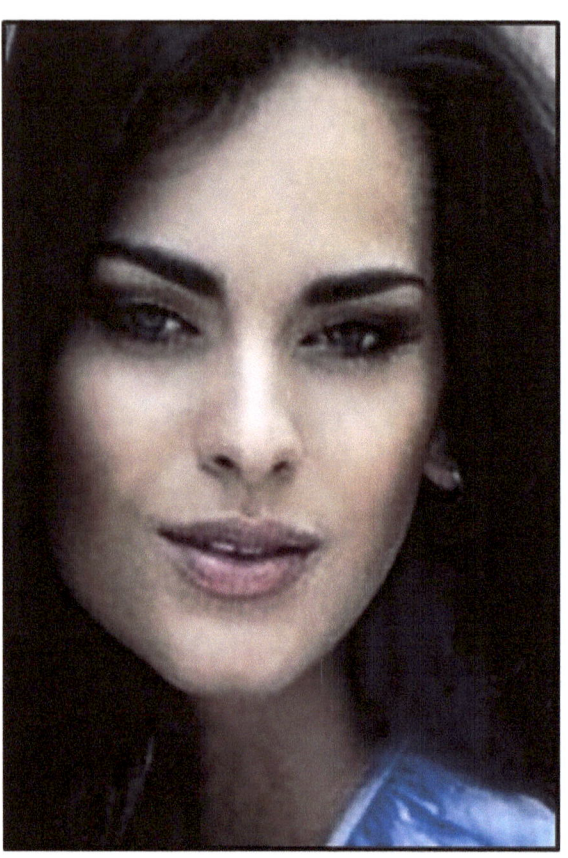
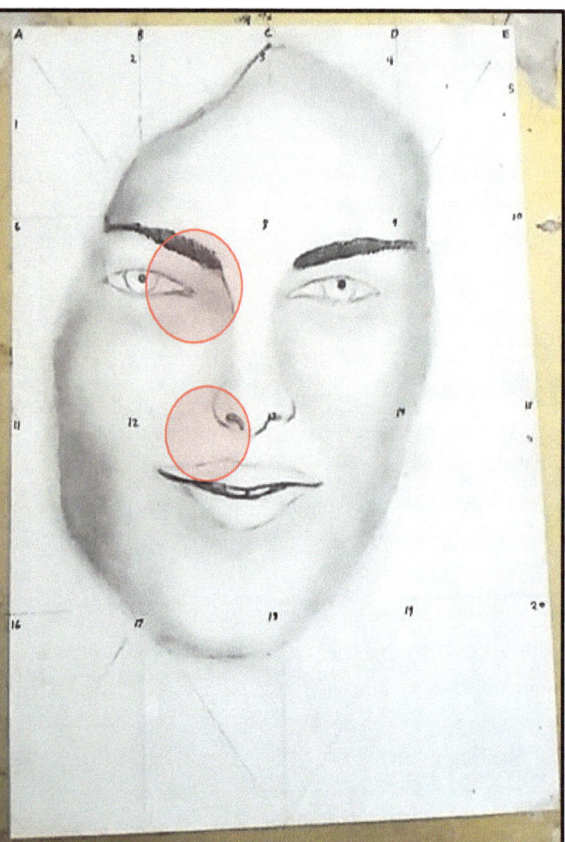

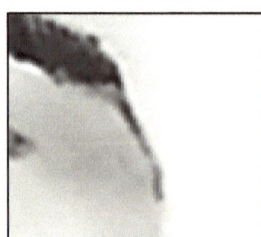
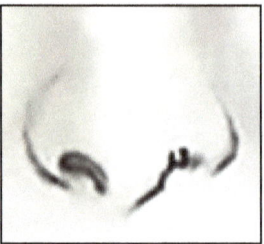
Before

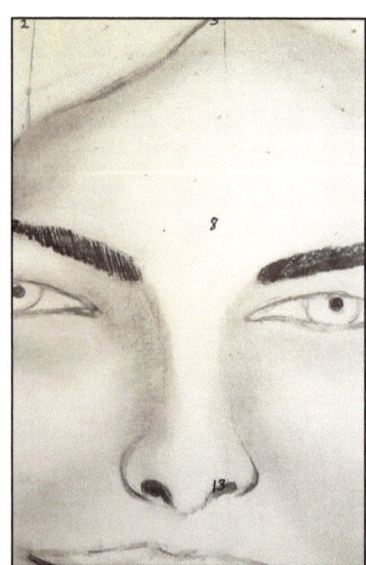
After

Lesson 4.0 Eye Details and Lips.

In this lesson we would do the details of the eyes and lips, also some detail shadowing in the nose area. But, I will not provide you with the details on where the dots should go. From herein forward you'll need to use the skills you have learned on your own, so you can practice and really start learning to do the art work.

On the lips you will do the shadowing on your own using the skills you have learned. However, I will show you how to do the pencil details on the lip. On the eyes I will do some pencil detailing and give pointers on how to fill in the eyes with details.

Step 1.0, on the eyes the model on the photo has use eyeliner to highlight her eyes. So, we add the highlight and also in this step we need to add the eyelids and eyelashes.

Here I am highlighting the areas you need to darken with darker pencil**.**

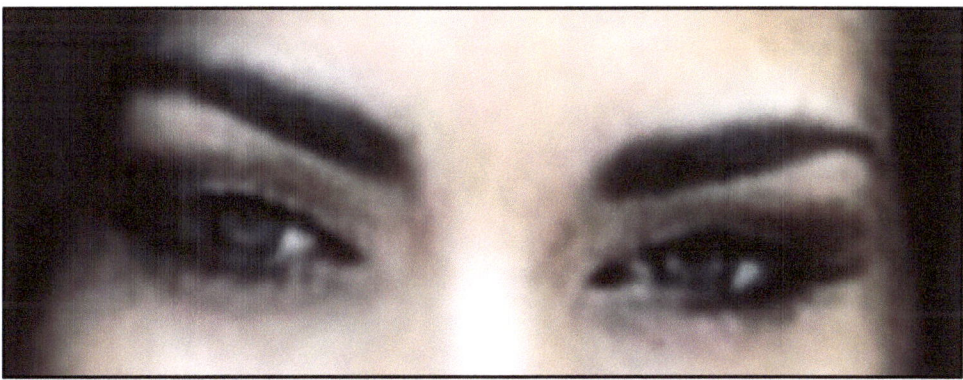

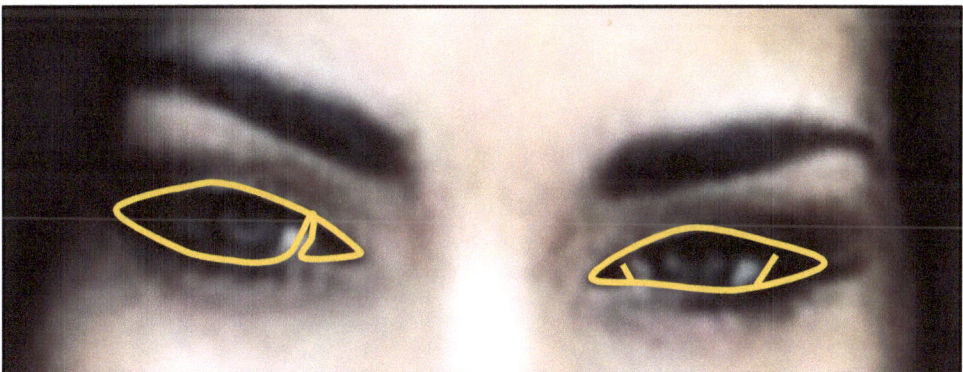

Lesson 4.0 Eye Details and Lips.

Here is what you should, if you're working a photo that is not this one we using here, just applied what is needed eye of your photo as you see it.

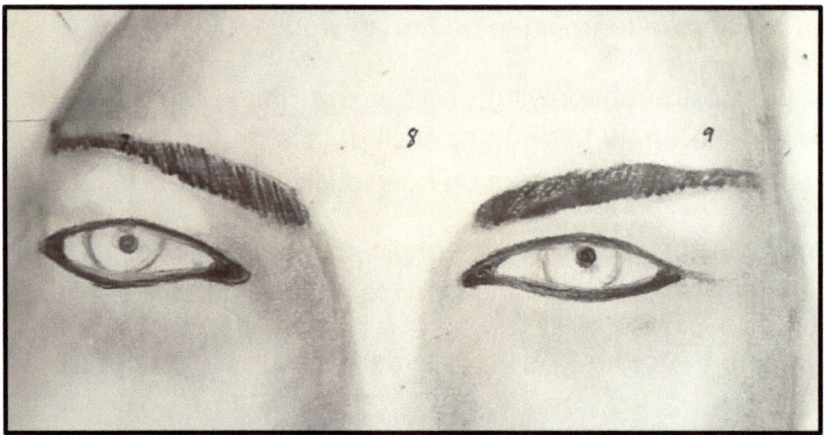

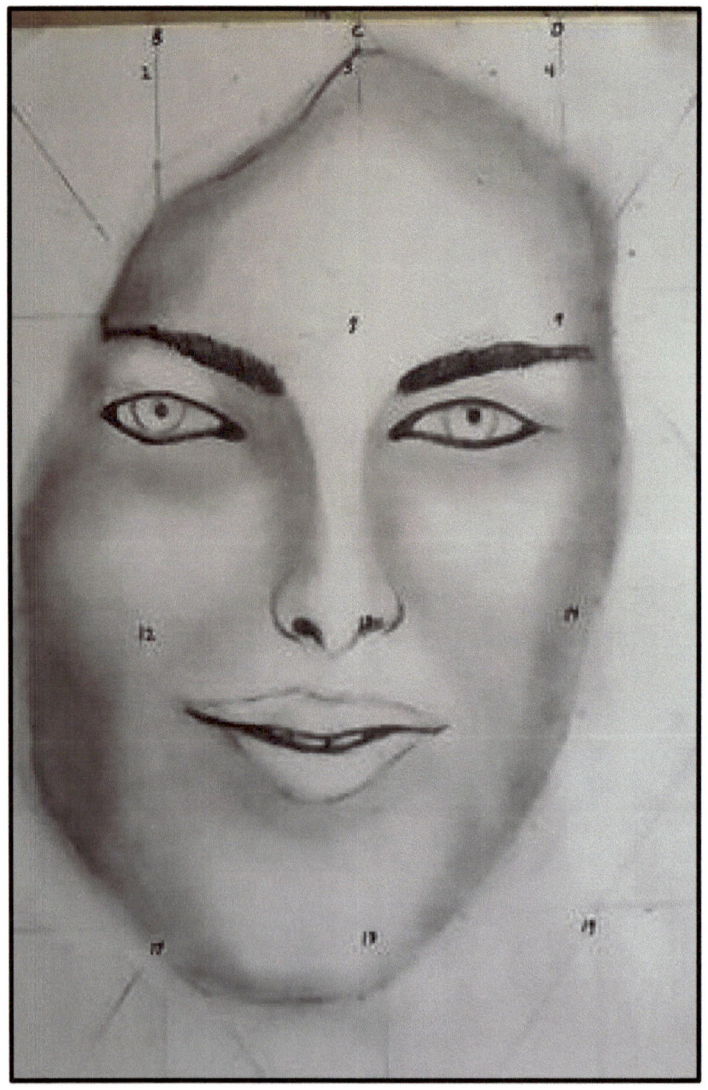

Lesson 4.0 Eye Details and Lips.

Step 2.0 we will detail the eyeball with your dark pencil, first you would add a light shading to the inside of the eyeball. If you look carefully at the eyes you'll see that the eyeball around the edges is dark. Make the darker edges only using a pencil and then fill in the eyeball shading with a pencil or your finger. But she has light eyes, so don't make the eyeball fill-in dark.

Drack line   **Shading**

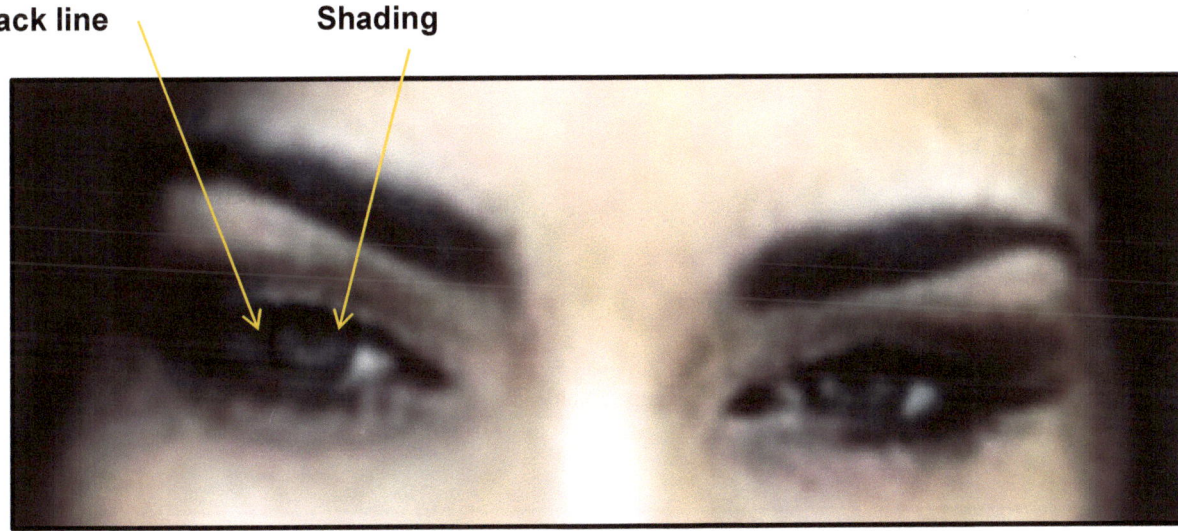

Here is how your eyes should look now.

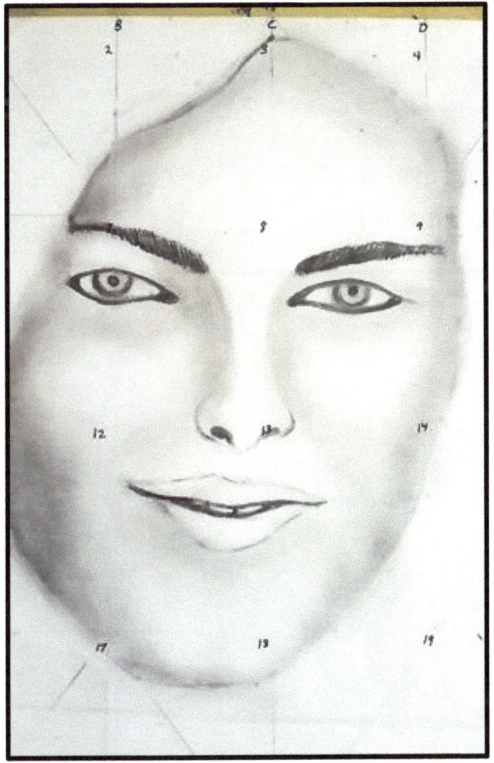

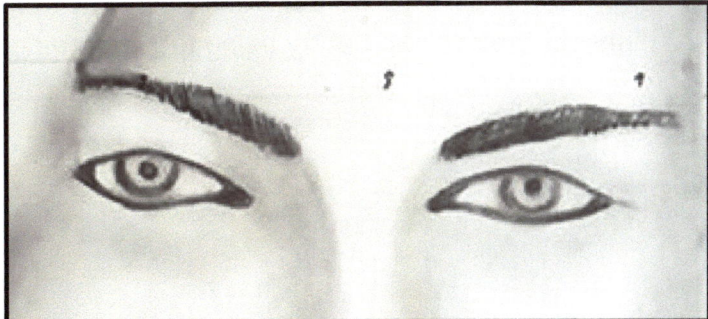

Lesson 4.0 Eye Details and Lips.

Step 2.0, here you would add the eye shade over the eyes, use your fingers to add these shades. Note; there is a bit of shade in the eye areas, so if your finger shades a little bit inside the eyes this is okay.

Shades

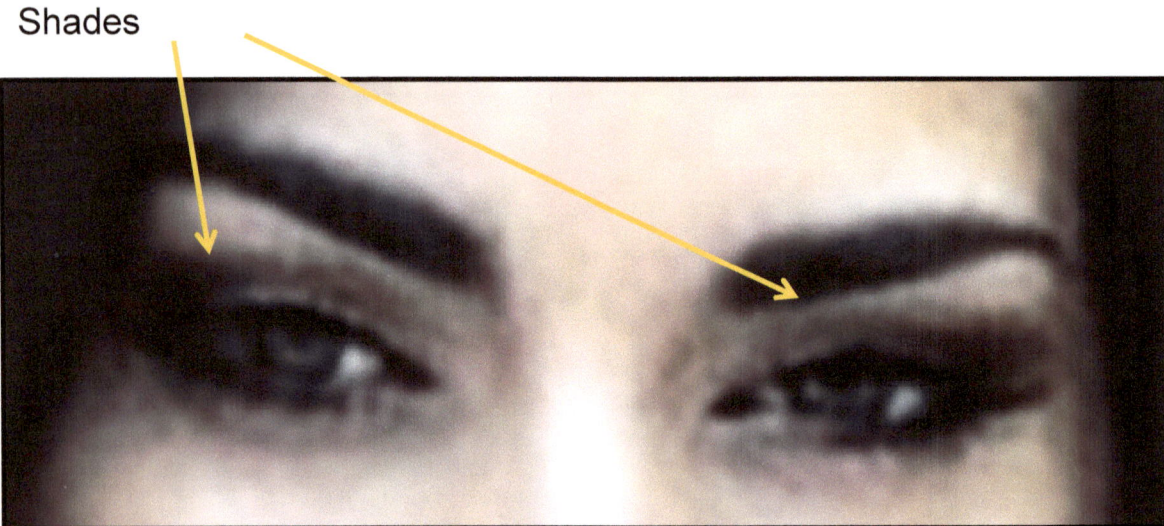

Lesson 4.0 Eye Details and Lips.

Step 3.0, now you would do the eyelids around the eye, you use the dots and line to help determent where the lines go. This you will do on your own, so you can learn how to place the dots and/or use the lines.

Look at where the eyelids are before you start drawing them. You can use your pencil to highlight the eyelids, but try using the light pencil to do the lines.

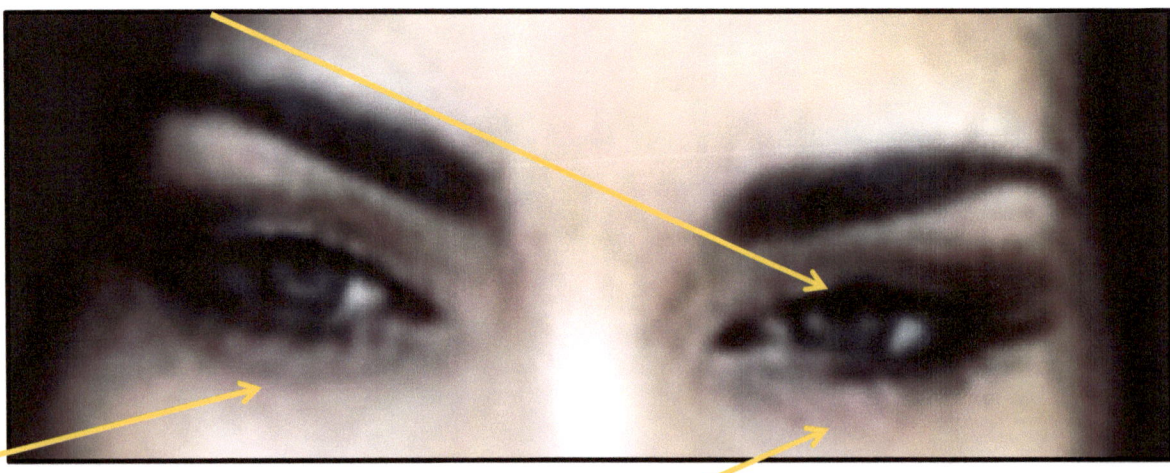

Lesson 4.0 Eye Details and Lips.

Here is how the eyelids and eye shadows should look like.

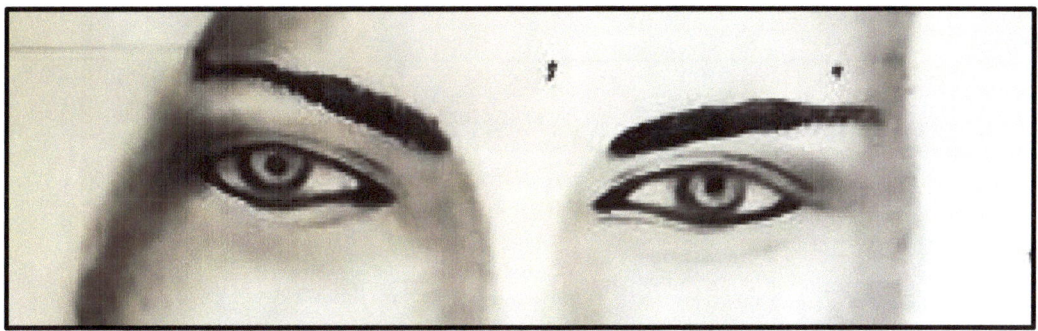

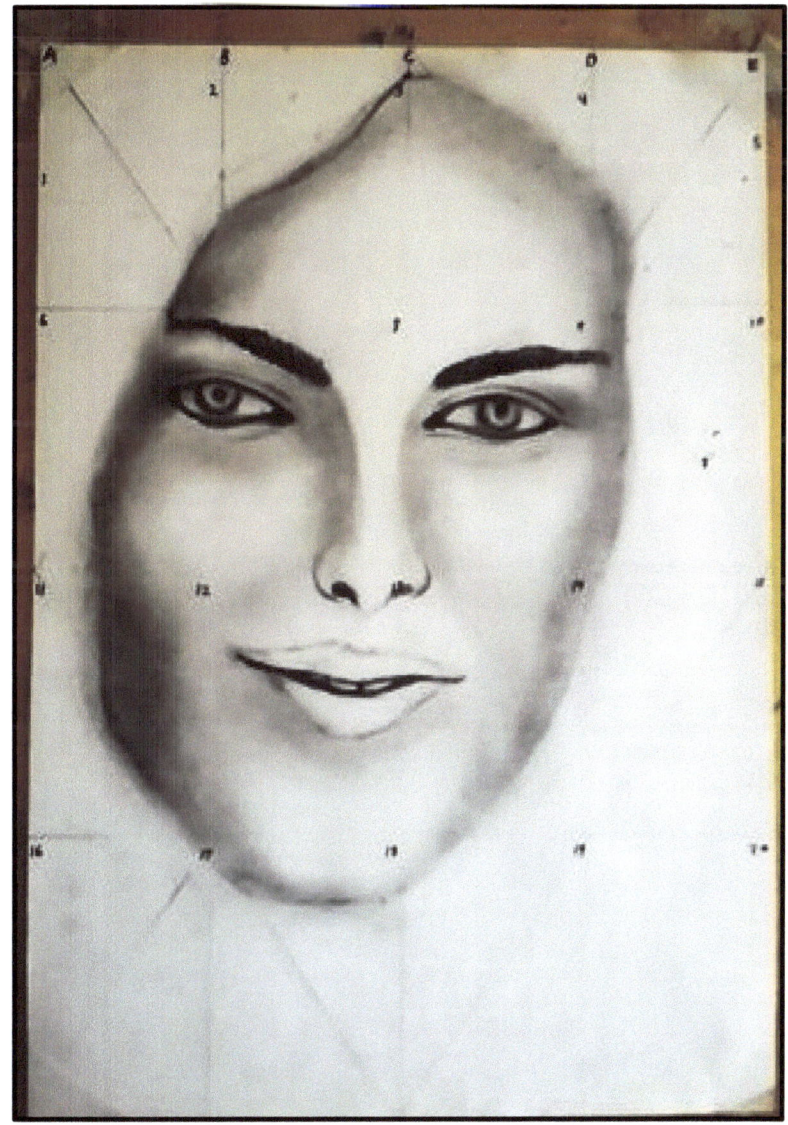

Lesson 4.0 Eye Details and Lips.

Step 4.0, now we will do the eyelashes on the top and bottom. Remember to use your dark pencil on the eyelashes.

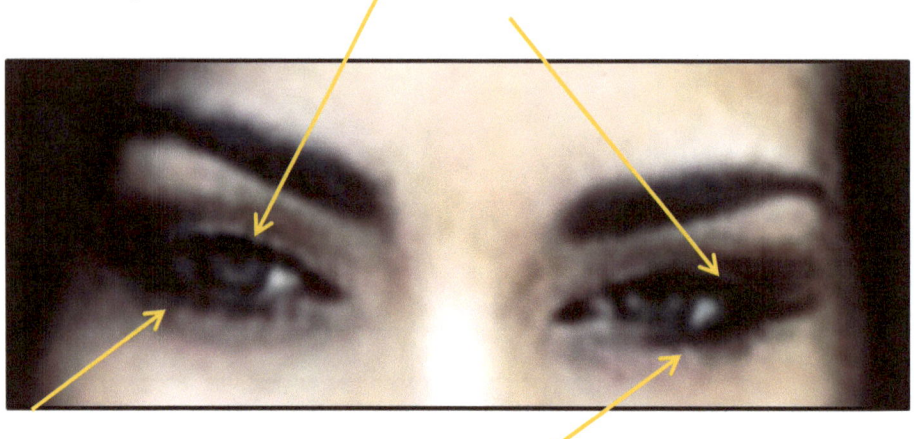

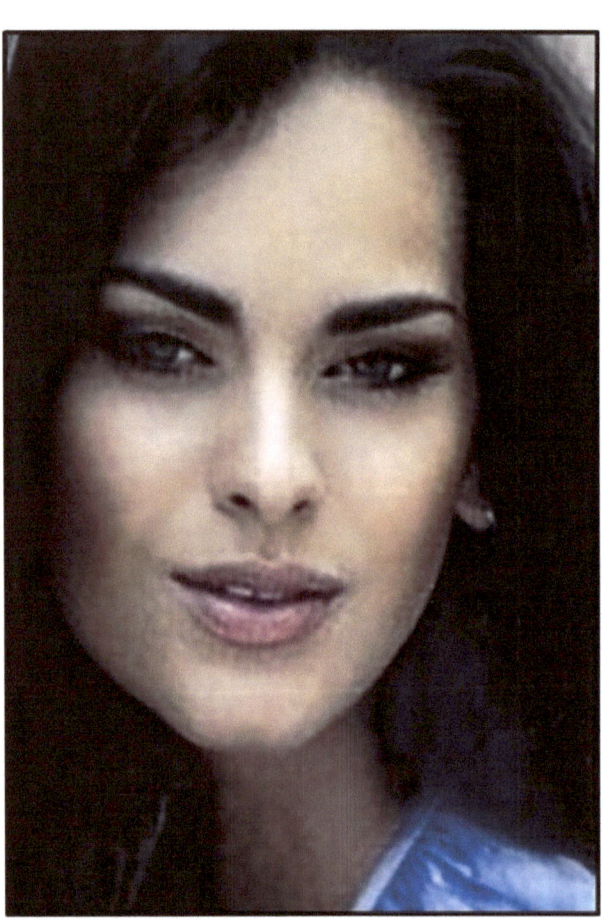

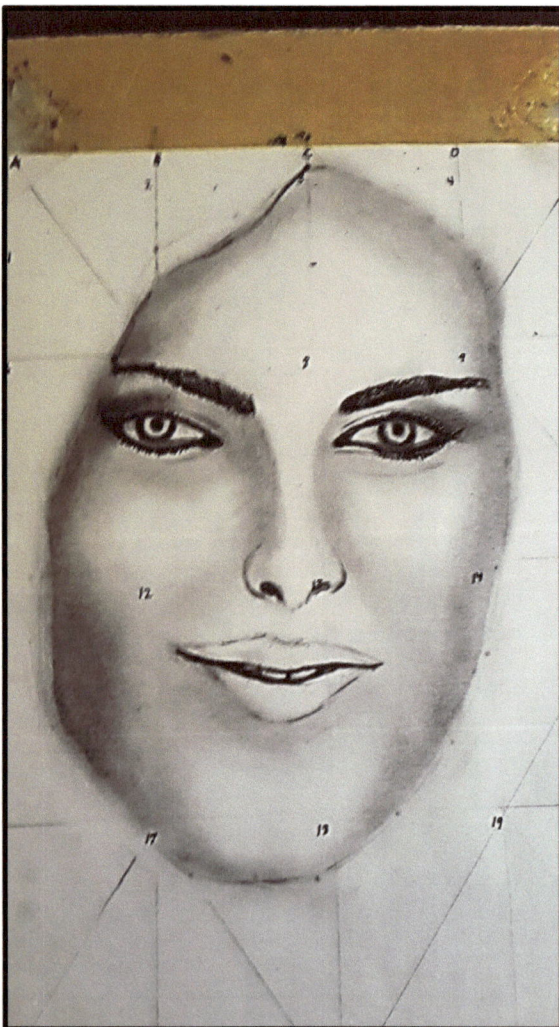

Lesson 4.0 Eye Details and Lips.

Step 5.0, now we will work on the lips details and on the shadows. We first will do the upper lip. Here is a technique that is not taught by many artists that involves the tip of an eraser you can see below. If you look at the top lip the edge looks almost white. This is in effect created by the shadow and the way we add this is by using the edge or tip of the eraser to do the highlighting work or the detail work.

Note; don't do this area until you have seen the photo on **Step 5.2.**

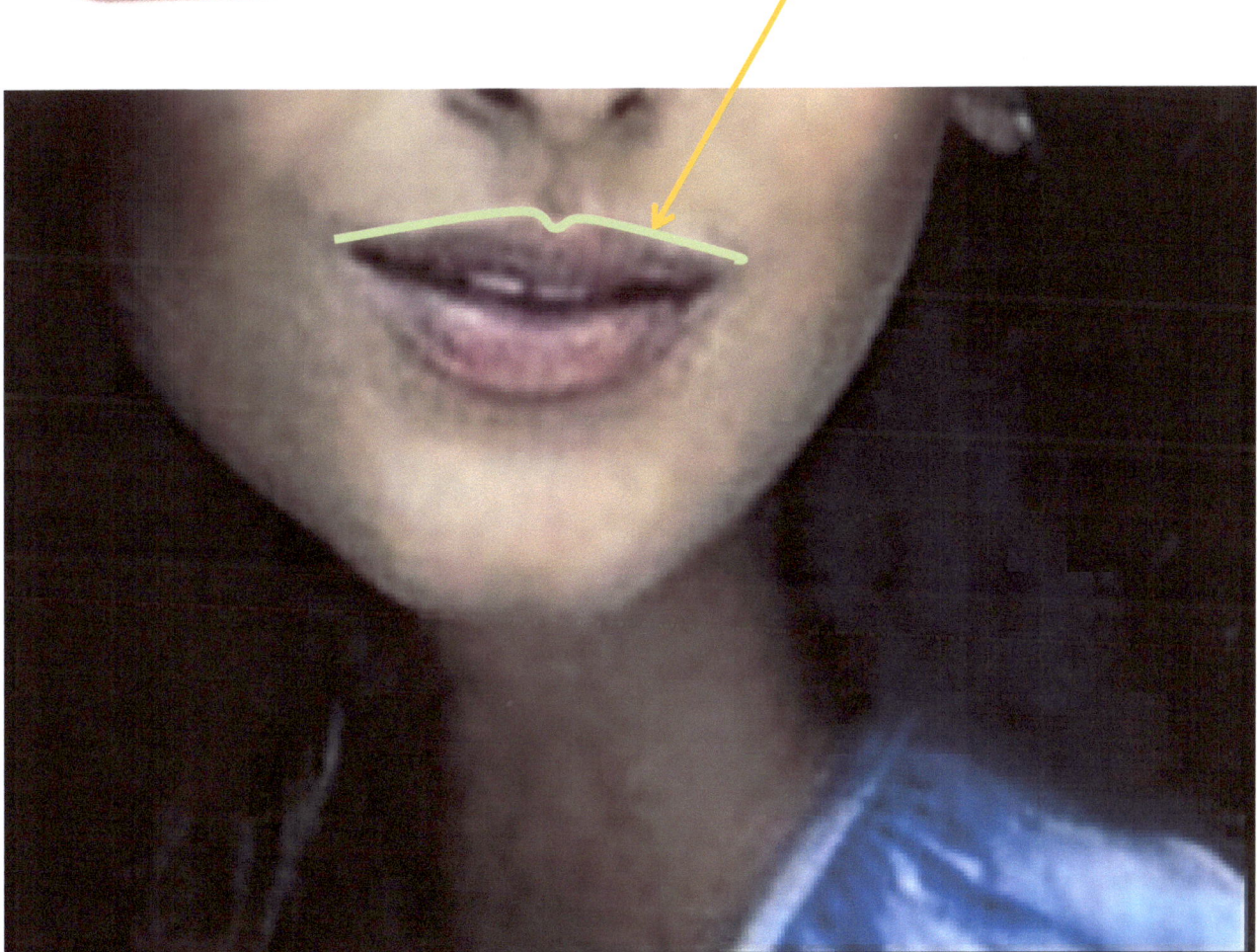

Lesson 4.0 Eye Details and Lips.

Step 5.1, first add the shadows to the top of the lip do not worry now about the highlight white that needs to be added with the eraser. Remember using the edge of your finger to fill in the shadows. I would advise you to use your small finger to do this. There is a shadow coming from the bottom of the nose to the top of the lip add this shadow and the other shadows on top of the lip. Also remember to use your blending paper to create shadow mix, so you can pick it up with your finger and added to the drawing. Note; if there are any lines, numbers, or dots, you must remove them before you add the shadows.

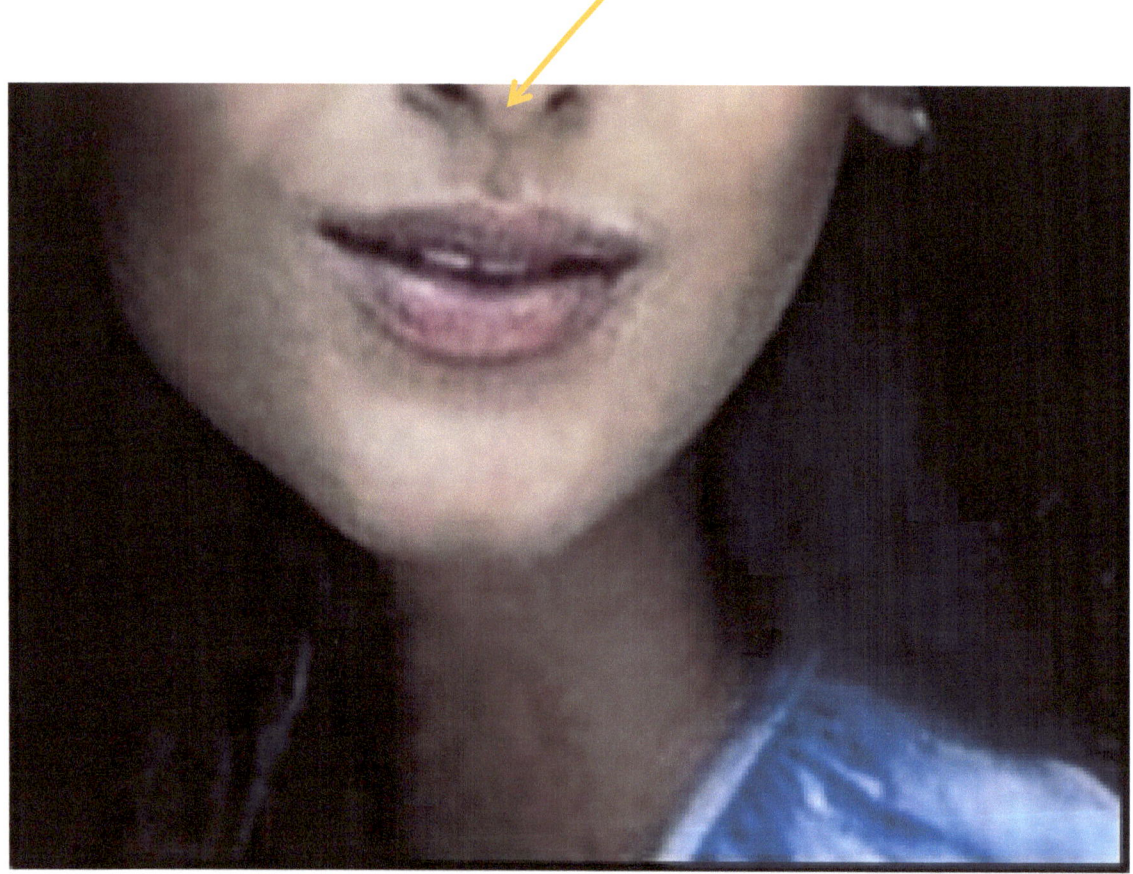

Lesson 4.0 Eye Details and Lips.

Step 5.2, now using the tip of your eraser as if it was your pencil you will then create this highlight over the lip and the highlights that come from the nose to the top lip.

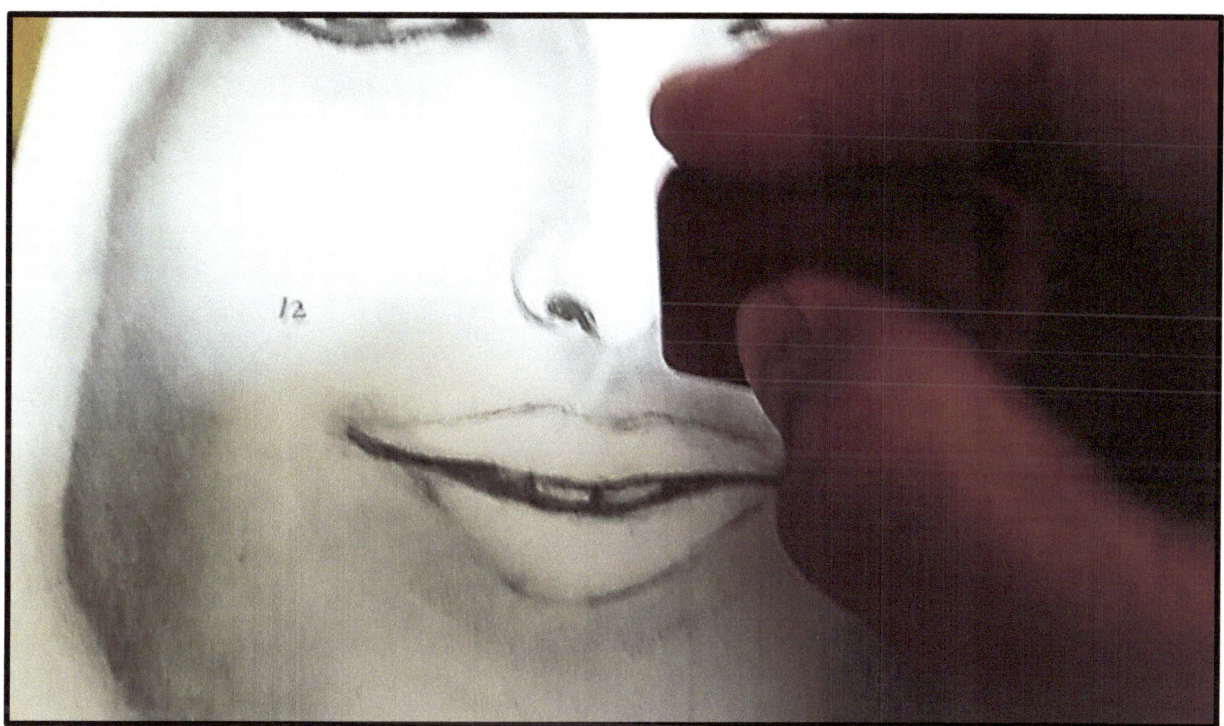

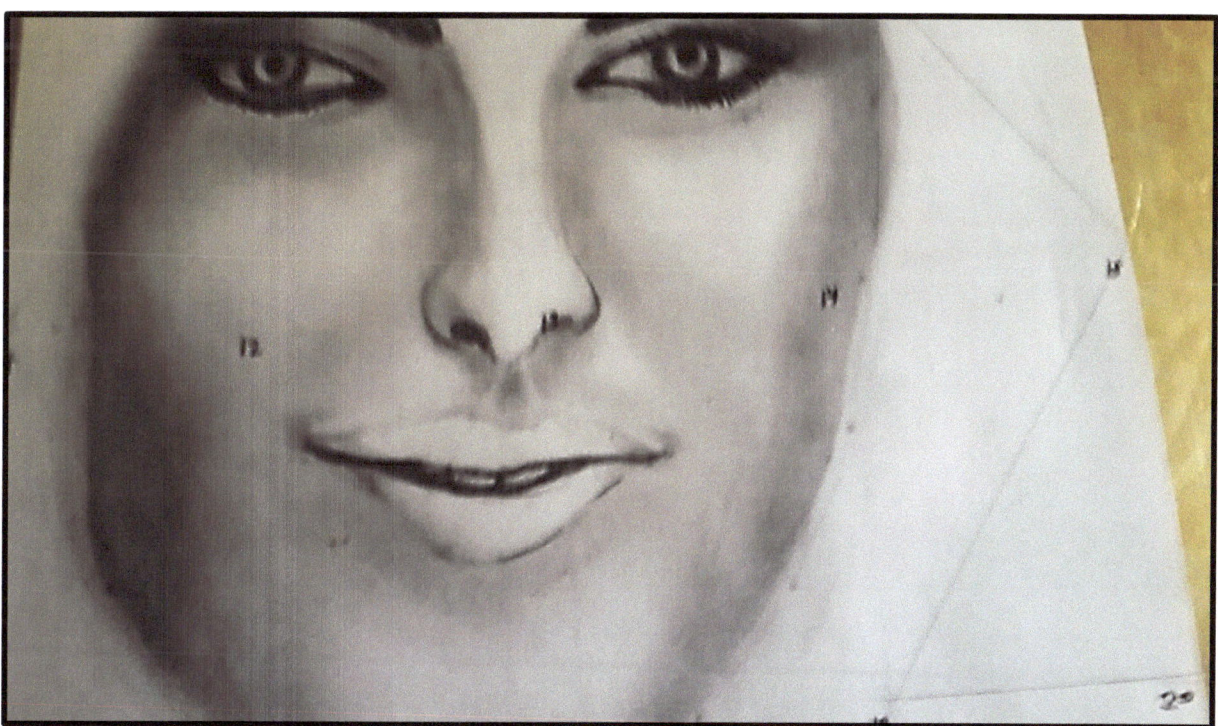

Lesson 4.0 Eye Details and Lips.

Step 6.0, now using your fingers add the shadow and coloring to the lips. Note; on the areas on the lip that has a shine or glare you would do the same thing as you did with the upper lip you will use the tip of your eraser to do the highlighting. So you first will fill in the lips and do the shattering on the lips and then you'll come back and do the highlighting with the eraser. For some of the darker areas you can use your pencil, but be careful not to make the line too obvious.

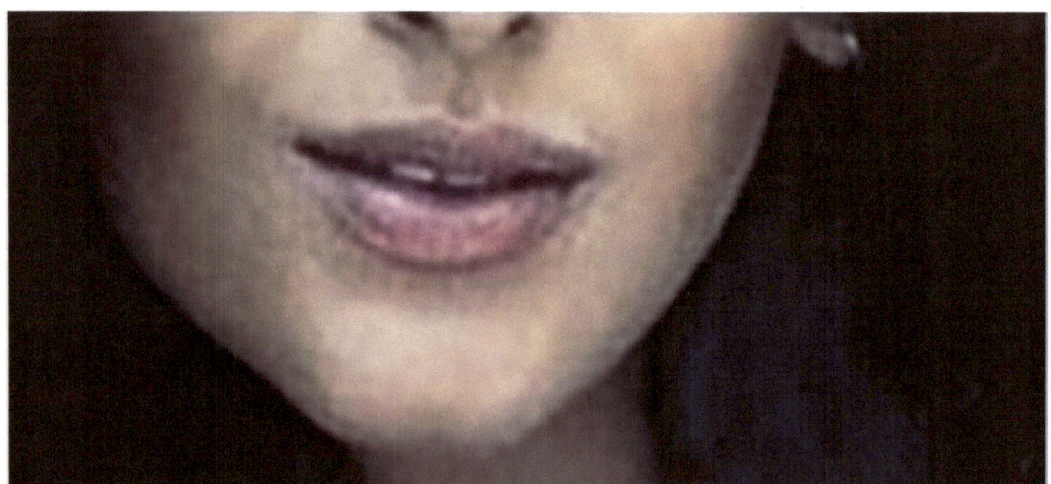

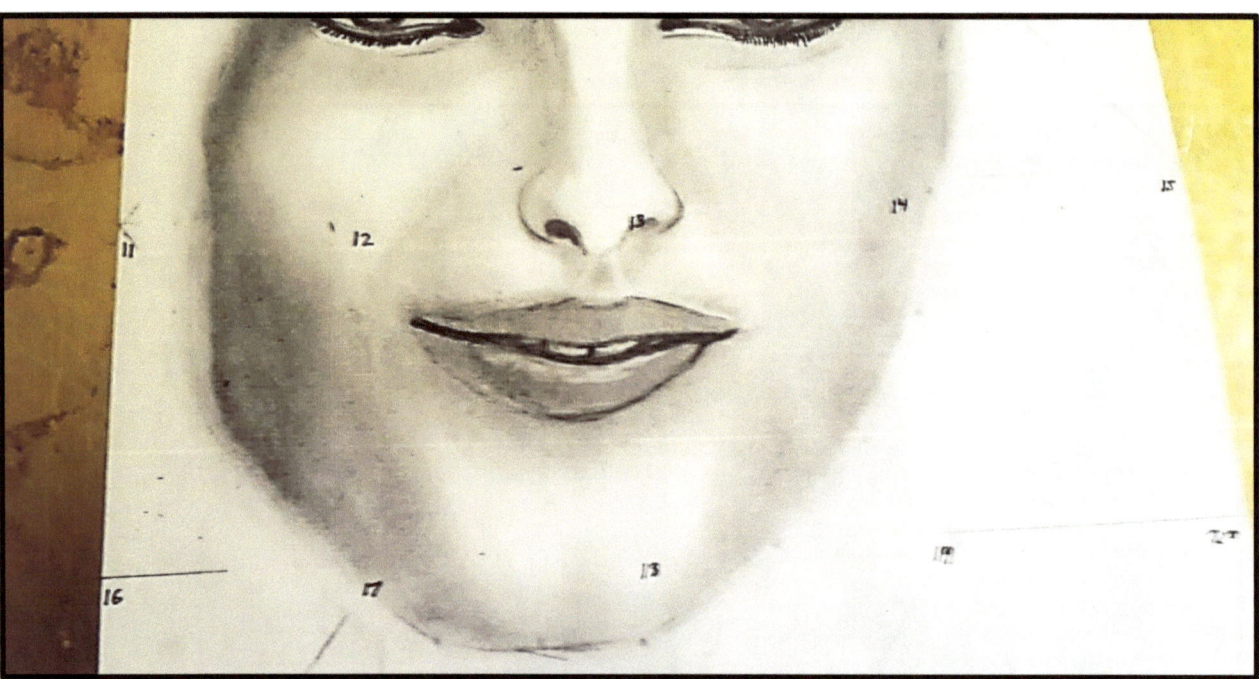

Lesson 4.0 Eye Details and Lips.

Before we move to step seven I will ask you now to review all your drawings and you're shadowing. Details and fix things as you think they should be fixed by either adding more shadow or removing some shadowing by lightly erasing areas or even adding more details to certain areas you might need.

If you have been doing the drawing from the photo on this book your drawings should looks similar to this.

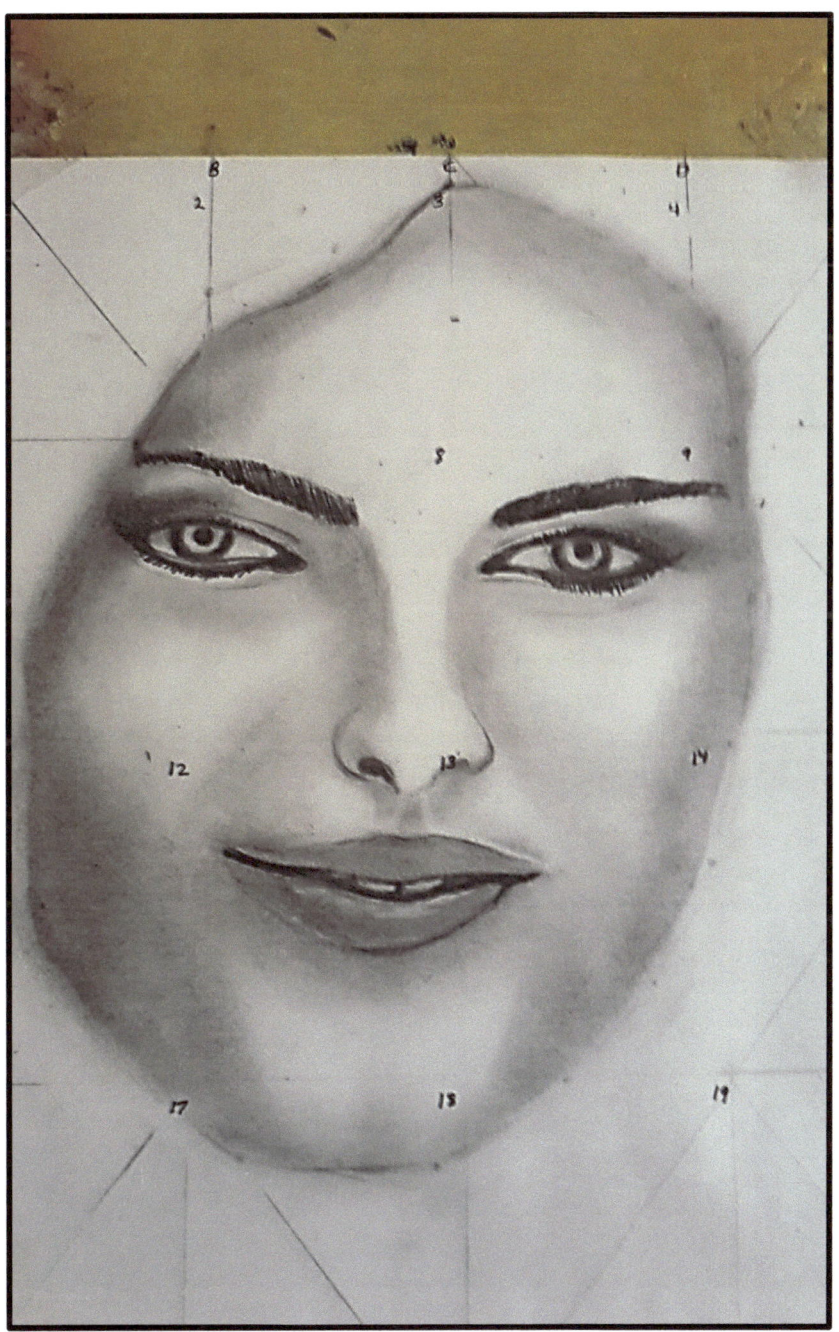

Lesson 5.0 hair and final details.

Step 1.0, on this step you have the option to complete the last detail on the face. Add the left ear using the skills you have learned up to now and it is not necessary to add the ear ring if it is more difficult for you.

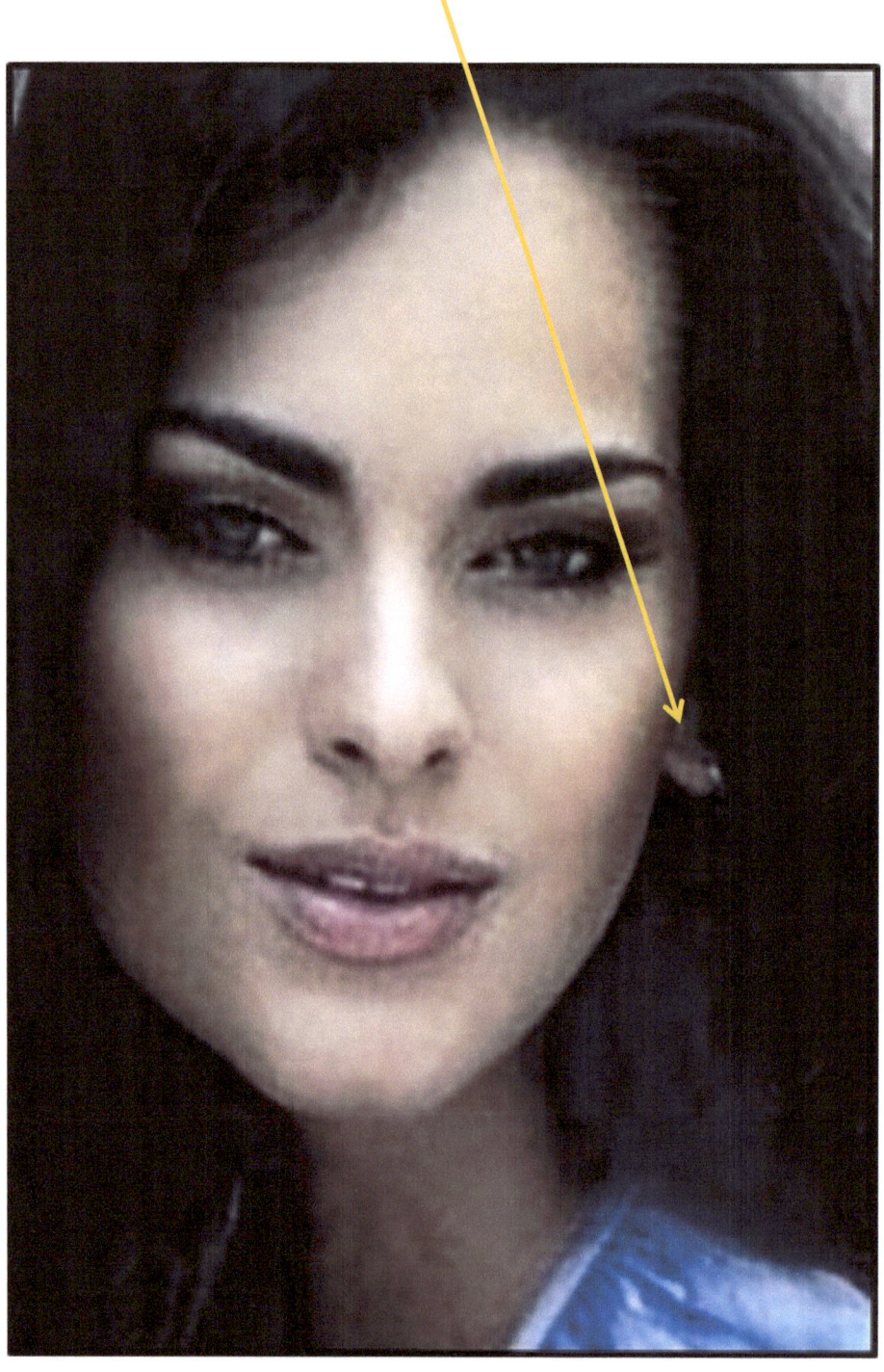

Lesson 5.0 hair and final details.

Step 2.0, we would now add the hair to her head however this is an option. The hair technique or techniques can be many. You can do the hair with a dark pencil you can also do the hair using acrylic dark paint, ink, charcoal sticks, watercolor, and other medias.

I decided for my drawing to use charcoal sticks. If you decide to also use charcoal sticks be careful in using the sticks, you should have some experience in applying charcoal sticks because you can make your drawing very messy very fast. You should be able to purchase charcoal sticks online from art stores or at good art supplies stores.

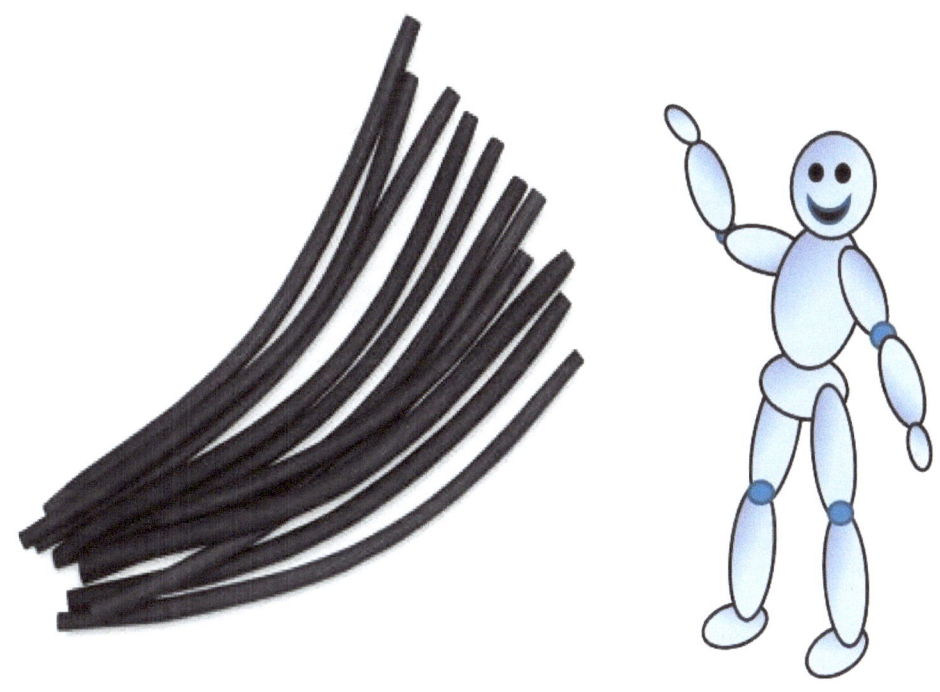

Lesson 5.0 hair and final details.

Step 2.1, the technique we will used to add the hair would be first to add the dark color of the hair and then do the highlighting of the hair using the tip of our eraser. Her shirt should be optional too, you can draw the shirt or you can cover it with hair.

Note; on the neck area there is a dark straight edge shadow that doesn't seem rights so I have opted to add my own style of hair in that area you made want to do the same.

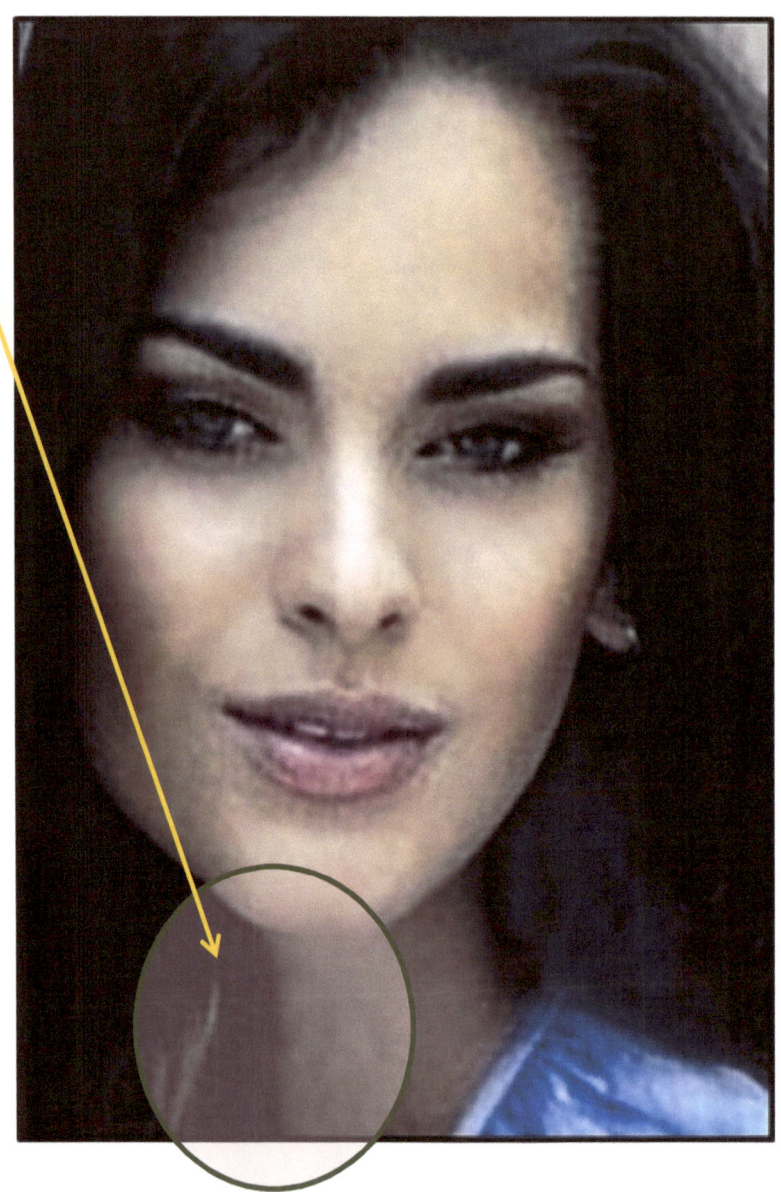

Lesson 5.0 hair and final details.

Step 2.2, we now will add all the dark areas of the hair by applying the charcoal stick. Note; charcoal sticks have different darkness and lightness, so in order to get a dark color sometimes you have to go many times over with the charcoal stick. Also note that charcoal stick can rub off, so once you have your drawing done you should add a special spray that is made for charcoal stick and pencil drawings that you can purchase at many of the art stores. The spray will prevent smearing of the artwork or prevent the drawing from getting lighter with time. But be careful when using these kinds of sprays and make sure that when you purchase the spray from the art supplier the supplier has good experience or has a good understanding for these kinds of sprays, because may be you can end up damaging your drawing or create glare spots on your drawing.

Note; when doing your hair you should follow the natural flow of the hair with your charcoal stick as if you were combing the hair by doing this you will give the look of the hair a more natural look. You will also be using your fingers to spread this charcoal and then highlighted with the charcoal stick.

Also note, when using charcoal stick not to have moister on your hands and to keep your hands dry, because if you don't you will surely have a mess on your hand that may end up on your drawing. So, remember to use tissue paper to set your hand on top and don't set your hand directly on top of the drawing. But, with charcoal stick it is possible to even spread the charcoal with a tissue, so be super careful when using charcoal sticks.

And one more note, because now you will be basically be finishing off your drawing you need to remove all numbers, dots, and lines in the areas you are going to apply the charcoal stick.

Also, at this time you must be super careful in erasing these lines, because you could tear up the paper.

Lesson 5.0 hair and final details.

Step 2.3, once you add the basic background color onto the hair you will use the tip of your charcoal stick to add the highlighters or details of individual strands of hairs, but don't go crazy in trying to add every single strand of hair. Just add some basic strands as you see on the photo that I have completed then you will add some highlights using the edge of your eraser or the tip of your eraser again following the contour or the flow of the hair.

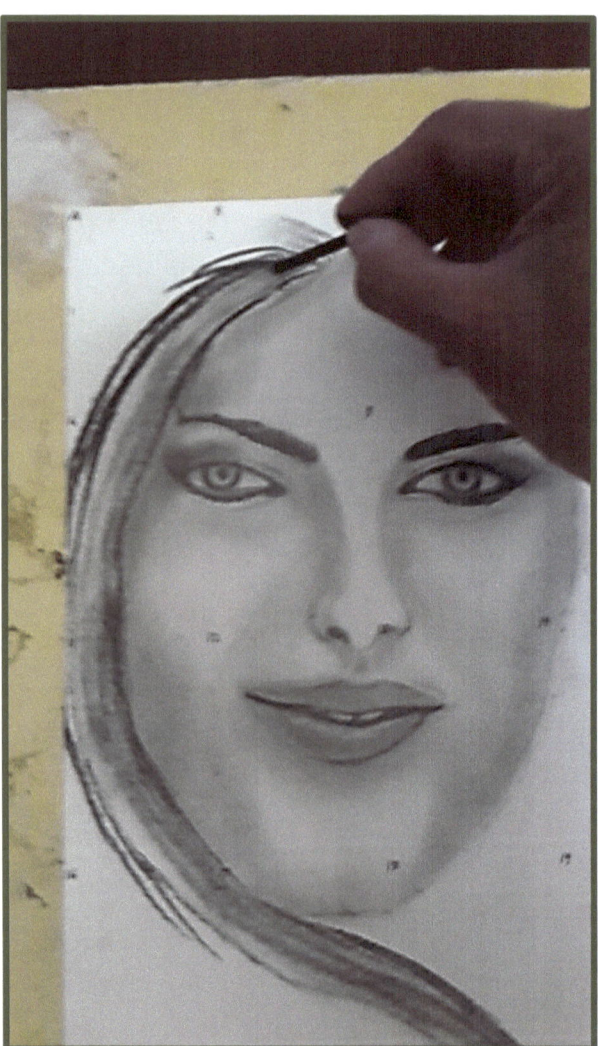

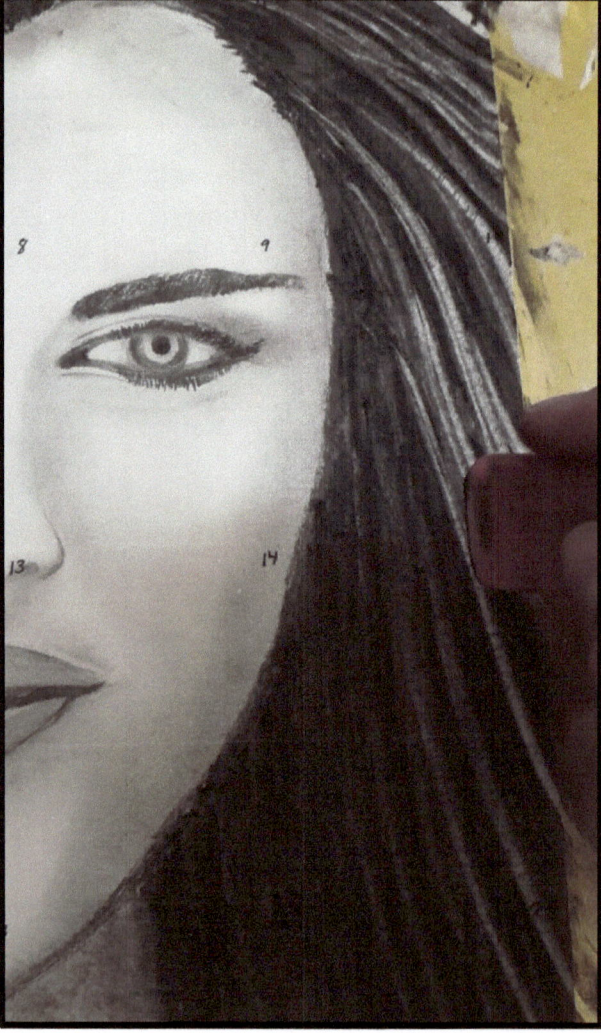

Lesson 5.0 hair and final details.

Step 2.4, once you're done your hair should looks similar to this, however this does take a lot of practice and you have to do more drawings and as time goes on you will get better and better both on your face and on the hair. But, for now you have the general platform on how to create a face by using the GDD techniques you have found within this book and have learned to use.

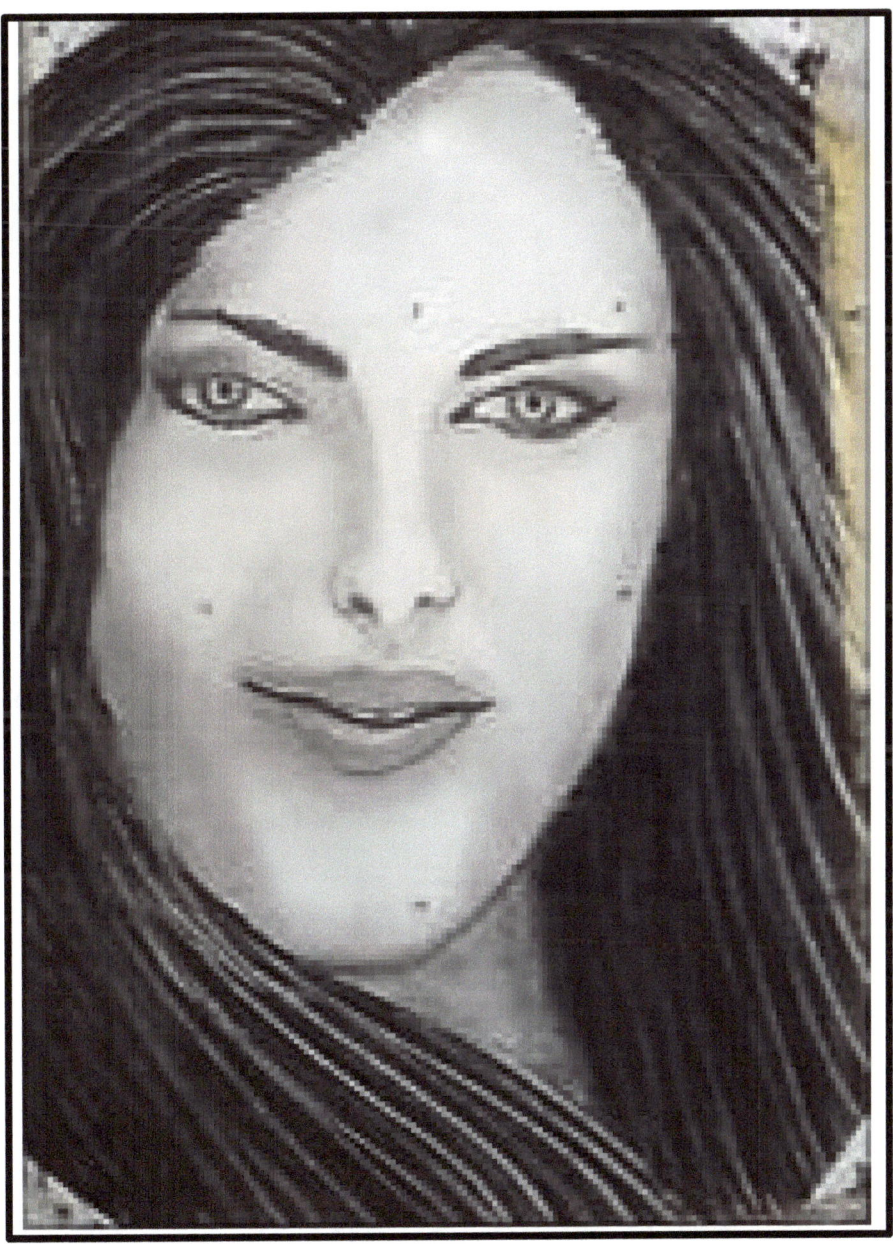

You are now finished with the drawing, but please read "Mistakes Part Two" on the next page to finish this book and get a better understanding on how mistakes can improve your drawing skills.

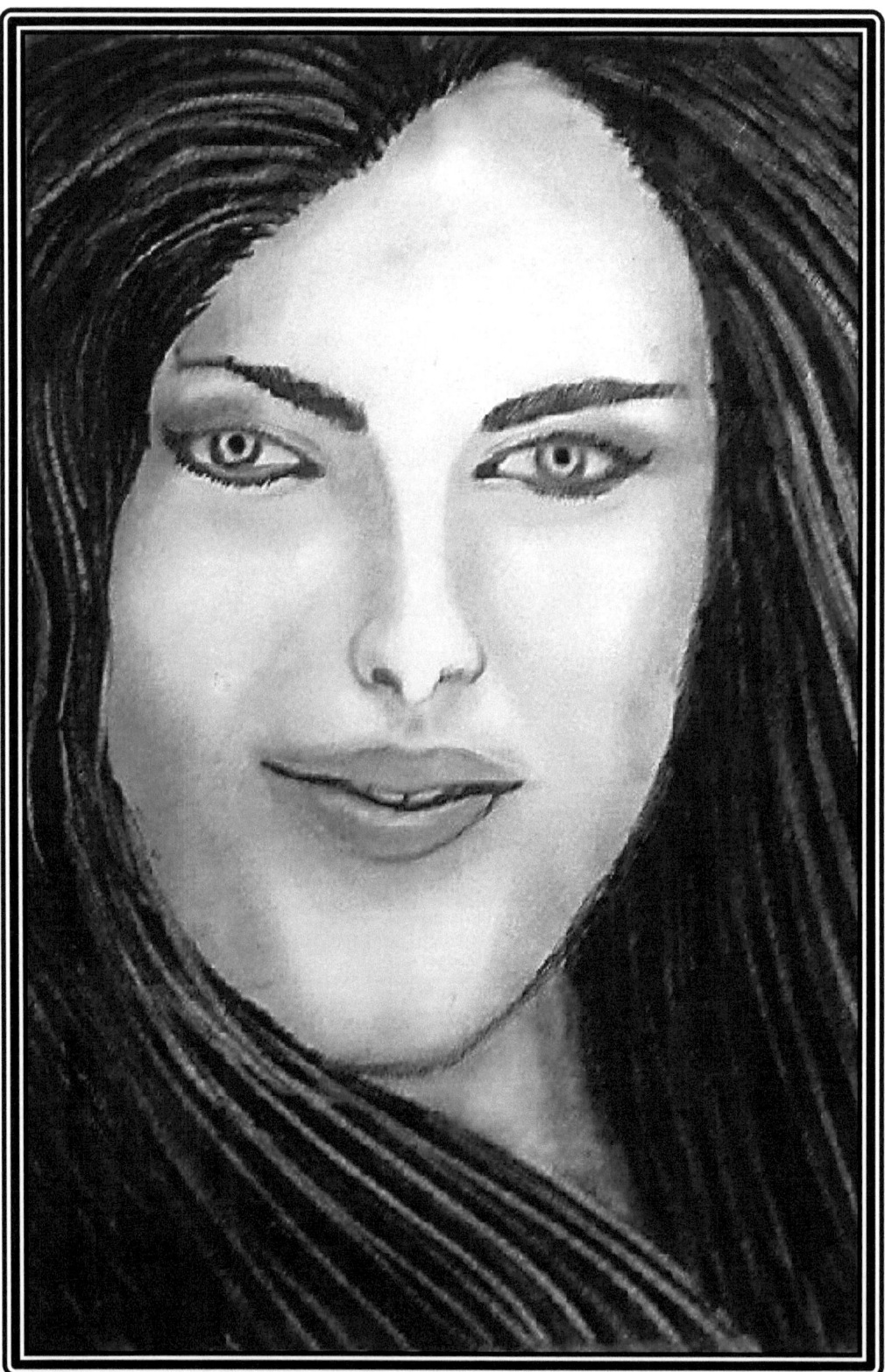

Mistakes Part Two

Here's an example how mistakes can make you a better artists. I believe some of you have seen on television shows or if you have attended art shows, artists doing some live incredible paintings or drawings within minutes.

I have seen on television on artists go up to a very large canvas and using a paint brush with black paint make an amazing painting of a famous person's face, but what was more amazing was that he did the painting upside down on the canvas and then after finishing turned the canvas right side up to reveal the face of the person.

I'm sure many people that seen this were amazed by the skills of the artists, but let me say most experience artists can do this.

This person who does these kinds of painting have practice many times to do the same painting over and over using one color and sometimes they use up to three or four colors to do the same painting over and over. Many times they started on a small canvas and then worked up to a large canvas on their way to making perfection. They may make many, many mistakes I'm sure with their artwork, but after practicing for a time and improving they made less and less mistakes on the artwork. They then continued to practice on till they can make the face perfect as they wanted and improved the speed or time it took them to complete the artwork. It was only then that they show the world their amazing art skills.

I am sure many people were totally amazed at the speed the artist made the painting of the face and were more amazed when he made the painting upside down. But, let me say that these artists that do these kinds of works didn't get to that level of skill by making no mistakes. It was only after making several or many, many mistakes and a lot of time practicing to make the same face and also learning from their mistakes were they able to obtain the skills they wanted.

So, if you make a mistake on a painting or drawing don't get frustrated this is normal. Many artists both beginners and professional artists make mistakes on their paintings or drawings and it will only help them to improve on their skills. Because, by recognizing the mistake you make, on your next painting or drawing the mistake will serve as the experience needed to improve the new artwork.

Sometimes I believe the best artists in the world are those artists who didn't allow mistakes to discourage them and use the mistakes as a learning tool to improve their artwork. So, if you want to devote yourself to doing artwork let your mistakes become a learning tool to improve your works and don't allow mistakes to become the tool of discouragement.

I finished the drawing on this book, but after finishing I notice there are mistakes in this drawing, but all these will do mistakes is improve my drawing capabilities on the next face drawing I do.

On the next pages see a mistake fix and see what the mistake was.

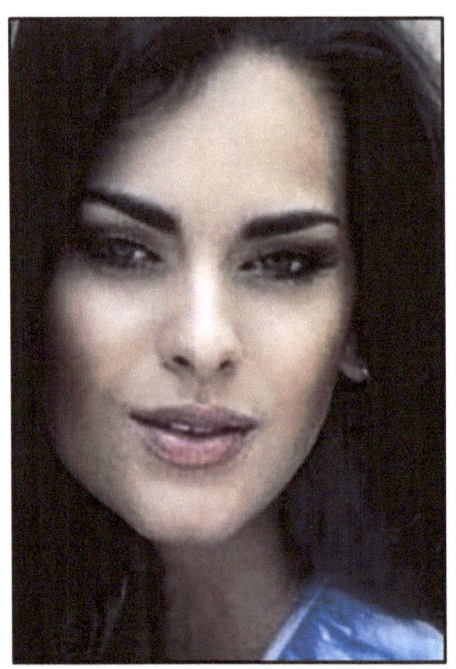

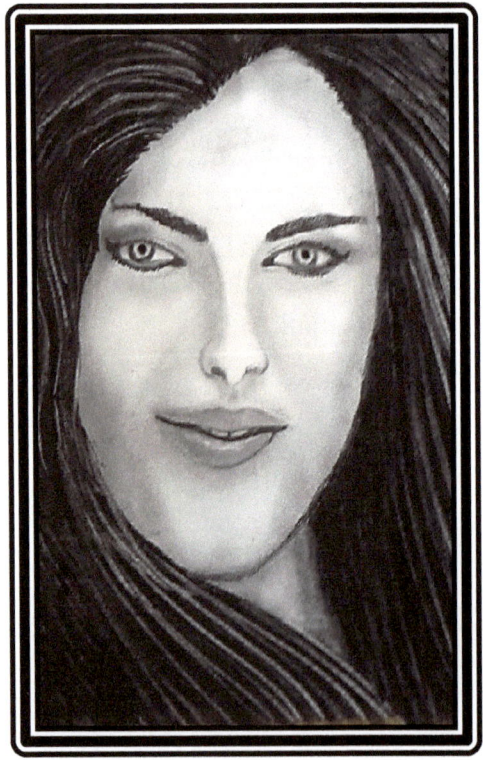
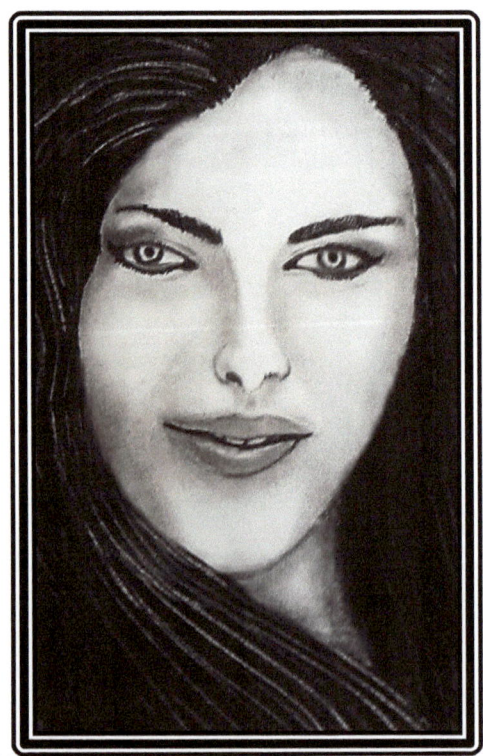

See a mistake...?

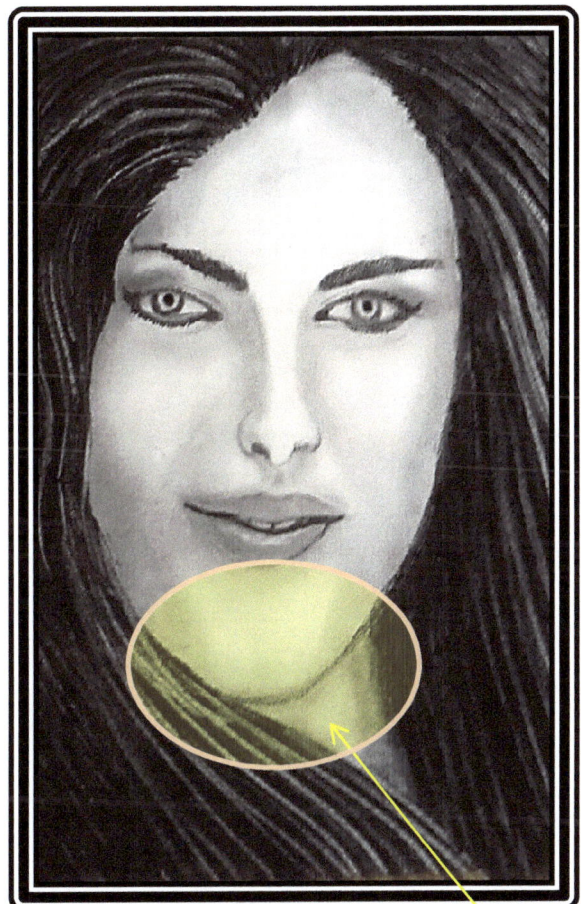

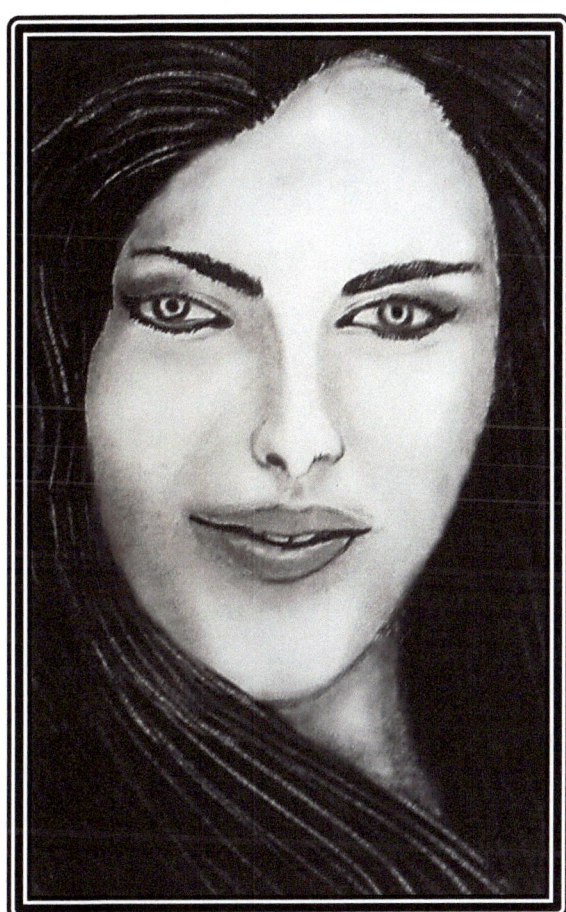

Fixed

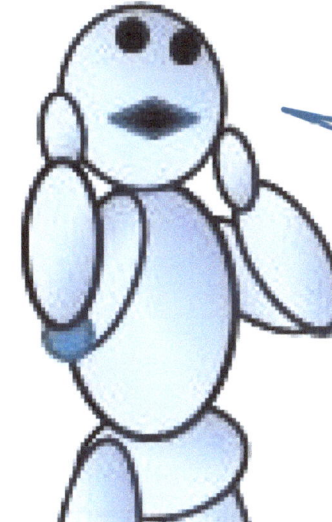

The jaw is too big

Thank you again and I hope you have enjoyed this book.

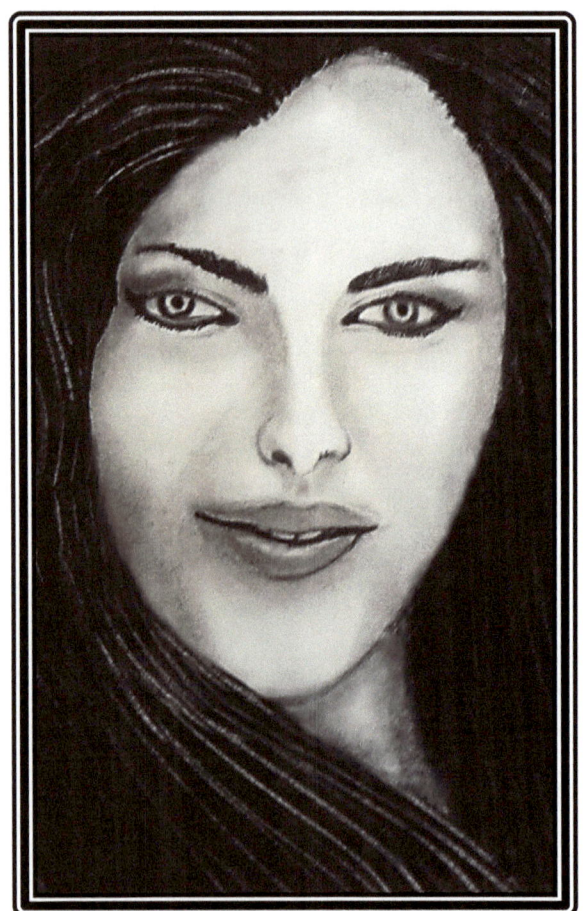

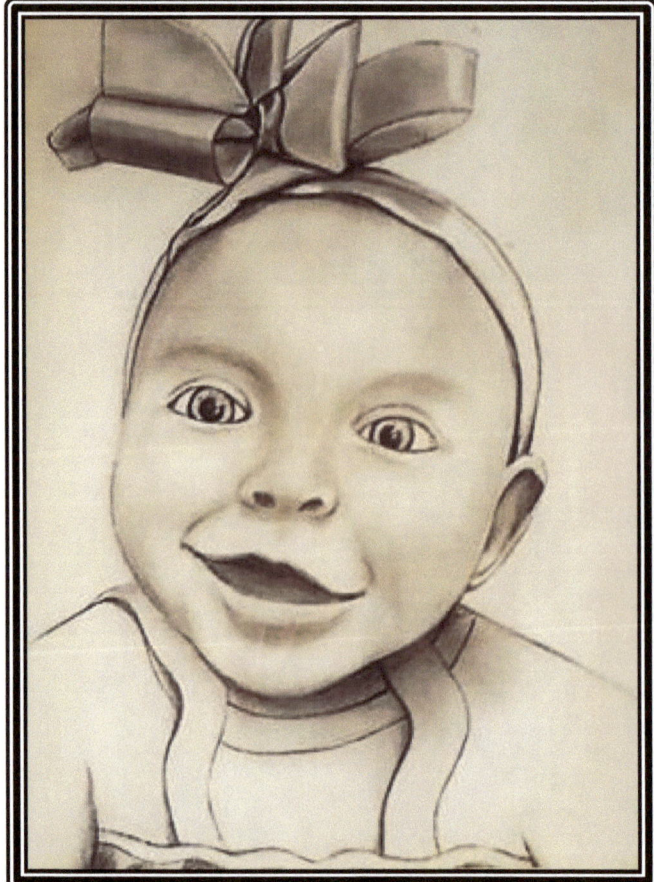

Jessie J. De La Portillo

www.ingramcontent.com/pod-product-compliance
Lightning Source LLC
Chambersburg PA
CBHW050741180526
45159CB00003B/1301